C000179100

INSIGHT INTO

ASSERTIVENESS

INSIGHT INTO

ASSERTIVENESS

Chris Ledger and Christine Orme

CWR

WAVERLEY ABBEY
INSIGHT SERIES

The Waverley Abbey Insight Series has been developed in response to the great need to help people understand and face some key issues that many of us struggle with today. CWR's ministry spans teaching, training and publishing, and this series draws on all of these areas of ministry.

Sourced from material first presented on Insight Days by CWR at their base, Waverley Abbey House, presenters and authors have worked in close co-operation to bring this series together, offering clear insight, teaching and help on a broad range of subjects and issues. Bringing biblical understanding and godly insight, these books are written both for those who help others and those who face these issues themselves.

Copyright © 2009 CWR

Published 2009 by CWR, Waverley Abbey House, Waverley Lane, Farnham, Surrey GU9 8EP, UK. Registered Charity No. 294387. Registered Limited Company No. 1990308.

The right of Christine Ledger and Christine Orme to be identified as the authors of this work have been asserted by them in accordance with the Copyright, Designs and Patents Act 8, sections 77 and 78.

All rights reserved. No part of this publication may be reproduced, stored in a retrieval system, or transmitted, in any form or by any means, electronic, mechanical, photocopying, recording or otherwise, without the prior permission in writing of CWR.

For list of National Distributors visit our website www.cwr.org.uk

Unless otherwise indicated, all Scripture references are from the Holy Bible: New International Version (NIV), copyright © 1973, 1978, 1984 by the International Bible Society.

Concept development, editing, design and production by CWR
Printed in China by C&C Offset Printing
ISBN: 978-1-85345-539-1

CONTENTS

INTRODUCTION

There are times when we can be too nice for our own good! Like most 'people-pleasers' we are often plagued by an overwhelming need to say yes to every request and end up looking after other people's needs to the detriment of our own. We're careful not to hurt the feelings of others by saying no, because we are really nice people, but we can then feel resentful towards those who make demands upon us. Keeping the lid firmly shut on our hidden frustration and anger when we are treated like doormats can lead to health problems. Sadly, we haven't learnt the importance of being assertive.

I first recognised my own people-pleasing tendencies when I started training as a counsellor. In spite of experiencing a loving, secure family, I had learnt to handle my dominant twin sister and mother (whose 'bark was worse than her bite') by means of the strategy 'peace at any price'. Being known as a people-pleaser was a badge I proudly wore. However, as I began to recognise that this behaviour was just as 'wrong' in God's eyes as being verbally abusive, I learned to change. My husband laughs when he remarks that I have became more assertive after my counselling training – quickly adding that this is a good thing!

Having counselled many people over the past twenty years, I have found that people-pleasing is like a psychological disease which can affect us in many distressing ways. Learning to say no where appropriate and developing assertiveness skills can be a tough task because first of all we have to identify the things that have kept us locked into this people-pleasing habit, and then learn a new language of relating. I hope this book will help you on your journey of understanding as you learn a new skill.

I am delighted that Chris Orme agreed to work with me in putting this book together, because as a friend and well-established author she has always encouraged me in all my writing.

We have changed names and some details of people's stories to preserve anonymity.

Chris Ledger

It has taken me more years than I care to admit to acknowledge that I have been a people-pleaser for a very long time. Helping with the school trip? Of course! Backstage at my daughters' ballet show? Naturally! Making mince pies for the carol service? Put my name on the list! Distributing boxes after the harvest service? Count me in! Delivering leaflets? Why not? Giving students Sunday lunch? Certainly! School newsletter for ex-pupils? Yes – well, someone has to … Fair Trade stall in the local supermarket? I'm up for it. Volunteers needed for something at church? My hand would be the first to go up (unless it was something I'm really hopeless at – like flower-arranging; even I wasn't daft enough to offer for that!). As time passed, I was no longer asked to help with school-related activities, but still there were constant requests for me to do all sorts of other 'worthy' things – and I couldn't say no.

I felt I had to say yes if *anyone* asked me to do anything legal – and even if they didn't ask personally, I felt obliged to sign up. Why? Well, I never really analysed the reason because, as I mentioned above, for years I was in denial about my lack of assertiveness. As a result I was often stressed and overtired and had no time for things that would renew and restore me. Slowly it dawned on me that I had problems in this area, so when Chris Ledger, a dear friend, asked me to co-author this volume with her, I jumped at the chance. This was partly because of the opportunity to see Chris (we are both so busy that we communicate mainly by email), but mostly because I recognised that I needed to be more assertive and felt this was an ideal opportunity to learn how!

Working through Chris's seminar notes, developing her ideas and relating them to the guidelines in God's Word have been such a blessing to me. I have come to understand where my people-pleasing habits originated and why, and as a result I am challenging my own flawed thinking in certain areas. I can already see a difference, both in my thinking and in the way I behave and react. I'm learning to be assertive without being aggressive – at last.

Christine Orme

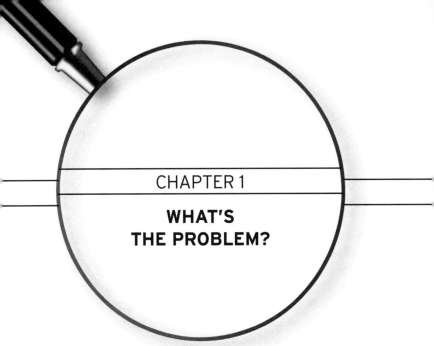

CHAPTER 1

WHAT'S
THE PROBLEM?

I've always felt the need to make people feel nice and warm ... at the expense sometimes of ... my own wellbeing.

(British actress Sienna Miller –
interview in *The Times*, February 2008)

Finding it hard to be assertive, to say no to other people's requests, or their sometimes unreasonable or inappropriate demands, is a very common problem. Type 'people-pleasing' into Google and you will instantly get approximately 4,630,000 references.

Do you find it difficult to be assertive? Are you a people-pleaser? Read the following statements and mark those with which you identify most closely.

- I feel guilty when I say no to requests.
- I feel obliged to please other people even when I know it will affect my health.
- I need to be needed so I'm nice to everyone, and can't say no.
- I feel anxious, even physically sick, at the prospect of confrontation and conflict.
- I feel I must never let people down, even when their demands are unreasonable.
- It's important to please people, to be accepted.
- I find it difficult to express constructive criticism because I'm afraid I'll make others angry and then not cope with their anger.
- I believe that good Christians are 'nice' people.
- I'm hooked on always doing things for others to please them.
- I feel worthless unless I am liked by everyone.
- I rarely delegate.
- I think I'm a bad person if I don't always please those around me.
- I believe it's important always to put others' demands and interests before my own.
- I never disagree in a meeting for fear that others won't like me, or will think me stupid.
- I have always needed other people's approval.
- I believe that conflict is bad and nothing good can come from it.
- I find it hard to express my true feelings to other people, in case they reject me.
- I realise that I fear people more than I fear God.

If you marked more than two of the above, you are almost certainly non-assertive. You find it hard to say no – to refuse a request from someone else – and you feel guilty if you do. You are, or you are in the process of becoming, a people-pleaser.

WHY CAN'T WE SAY NO?

We shall come back to this question a number of times, but one of the main reasons why we find it difficult or even impossible to say no is because of *fear*. We fear the possible consequences of saying no: we are afraid of being rejected, or of causing pain to others; we are afraid of feeling guilty; we fear conflict, afraid that other people will be angry with us if we say no to a request. We fear that not pleasing people will mean they don't value us; we're afraid that if we don't do what others want we are worthless people. And the result? Something within us drives us relentlessly to please other people at the expense of our own health and wellbeing.

CONSEQUENCES OF BEING UNABLE TO SAY NO

There are two aspects to this: the more obvious is that we find ourselves constantly saying yes to others' demands or requests and thus feel out of control because of the pressure on our lives; a less obvious, but nevertheless very real, aspect may be that we get to a point where we can't say no to the demands we are placing on *ourselves*. It was a long time before Chris O finally recognised this and made a conscious decision to take some time each day to do something she *wanted* to do, rather than driving herself to do all the 'worthy' things she thought she *ought* to be doing. The following are other consequences of being unable to say no:

- I take on too much resulting in exhaustion and, eventually, 'burnout'.
- I don't ever say what *I* want, so finally reach a point where I don't even *know* what I want!
- I tell 'little white lies'.

- I feel I have to 'rescue' others.
- I allow others to impose their will on me.
- I feel I have to protect others from pain (even if doing so causes *me* pain).
- I suppress uncomfortable feelings of fear, anger and guilt.
- I am left feeling frustrated with myself.
- My most important relationships are affected.
- I lose touch with the person God wants me to be.
- My behaviour becomes self-defeating:
  - I say yes when no would be more appropriate.
  - I please others because I want to be thought of as 'nice'.
  - I become a compulsive people-pleaser.
  - I adopt a philosophy of 'peace at any price'.
  - I pretend to be calm or OK when inside I'm really angry.

BOUNDARIES

One reason why some of us have difficulty in being assertive and saying no to unreasonable demands or inappropriate requests is that we have difficulty in setting or keeping boundaries. What do we mean by that?

We see boundaries everywhere: fences, hedges and walls around gardens, fields and parks, moats around castles. They spell out a message: 'The area within this boundary is my property or territory.' In our emotional and spiritual world, boundaries are just as real but often harder to see. They define us, identifying where we end and someone else begins, and they help us to know what we own and hence for what we are responsible. We are responsible *to* others and *for* ourselves. Boundaries therefore help us to distinguish our property. (If you find this concept difficult, try using the word 'limit' instead of boundaries.)

Most boundaries are not impenetrable: castles have moats and walls, but they also have drawbridges and gateways; fields with fences round them have gates, and houses without doors would be useless. Boundaries, as Drs Henry Cloud and John Townsend, who have written several books on the topic, point out, are to 'keep the good (or the desirable) in and the bad (the undesirable) out'[1]. We can see how this applies in the visible world: the walls of our homes offer us protection and safety in our family life; they keep out intruders – those who would steal and destroy.

One of the best and most basic ways of maintaining our spiritual and emotional boundaries is by saying no. We have to say it to our children as they grow up and explore – and don't they test the boundaries we set!

WE SAY NO:
to keep them safe:
- Don't touch the hot stove.
- Don't play with the sharp knife.
- Don't go near the edge.

or to maintain our sanity:
- No, you can't get up and come downstairs; it's bedtime and Mummy and Daddy need some space and quiet.
- No, Mummy has a headache so you can't play your drum now.

or because it will throw our schedule:
- No, I won't take you to the park right now – I have to get dinner.
- No, you can't watch your *Bob the Builder* DVD now because we have to take your sisters to school.

or because it could spoil something of value:

• No, you can't play with my special necklace because you might damage it.

If we can set and maintain boundaries with our children, why do we find it so hard to say no to others? We sometimes speak of people 'trampling' all over others, and people who have difficulties in maintaining their boundaries – in other words, people who find it hard to set limits – are in fact letting others into their territory, their garden, and allowing them to trample all over the flowers and plants of their inner world. Another word for people who can't set boundaries by saying no is 'non-assertive'.

JESUS

As we look at the life of Jesus we see that He set boundaries. He *could* say no. He could be assertive, doing only what His Father wanted Him to do (John 5:19) rather than being pulled this way and that by the demands of individuals and crowds. If we are prone to people-pleasing we sometimes give in to 'the tyranny of the urgent': someone asks us to do something for them and they want it done *right away*. They imply that we really have to drop everything and do it *now* – and we do, even though we may have been doing something important or legitimate for ourselves. Jesus was never at the mercy of 'the urgent'; when He was asked to go and heal Jairus's daughter, who was dying, He set off with Jairus through a great crowd that had gathered to see Him. As He moved through the crowd He realised that someone had touched Him for healing. Although He knew that person had been healed because power had gone out of Him (see Luke 8:46), he stopped, realising that the woman in question needed more than just the physical healing of a chronic haemorrhage; she also needed His compassionate love and affirmation: 'Daughter, your faith has healed you. Go in peace' (v.48).

WHAT IS ASSERTIVENESS?

Assertiveness is the ability to express one's thoughts, feelings and desires in a way that doesn't abuse others. It is appropriate, direct, honest and open communication and, most importantly, *assertiveness is a skill that can be learnt.*

Learning to be assertive will help us to grow in self-confidence and will enhance our relationships because it gains respect from others. Assertiveness helps maintain the healthy view that in God's sight we are all of equal worth. This means that others are not better or worse than we are, but that we are all equally deserving of being listened to and having our preferences considered. In short, assertiveness allows us to state our own needs and desires, whilst at the same time acknowledging that those of others may be of equal importance.

Many people – particularly women – find it difficult to be assertive without first working themselves up into a state of aggressiveness. They confuse the two, believing that assertiveness means standing one's ground, arguing a point and winning. However, assertiveness is not about winning or losing. Rather, it's about finding a compromise so that the end result of any difference of opinion or conflict is a win/win situation, not a win/lose one. Assertiveness comes midway between passivity (being a 'doormat') and aggressiveness. We might summarise the results of the three positions as follows:

• Aggressiveness resorts to bullying tactics and destroys relationships.

- Passivity avoids conflict of any kind, but at a price – it leaves the passive person with a sense of deep-seated helplessness, powerlessness – and sometimes hopelessness too. Indeed, the passive person, because they do not know how to express their anger appropriately, may cope with it by 'stuffing it down', letting it turn into resentment and bitterness.
- Assertiveness builds self-confidence, releases us to be the people God has made us to be, enhances relationships and reduces conflict.

AGGRESSION	ASSERTIVENESS	PASSIVITY

✕━━━━━━━━━━━━━━━━━━━━━━━━━━━━━━━━━━━━━━✕

Where do you think you come on the Aggressiveness to Passivity scale? Remember that although we can learn to be assertive, some of us may find it harder than others and may need a lot of practice!

EXERCISE

Read through the scenarios below and identify, by ticking the appropriate box, whether the response is aggressive, passive or assertive. Then ask yourself, 'How would I respond in that situation?' and decide what kind of response you have identified as your own.

SCENARIO A

At 4.30pm, only half an hour before John is due to finish work, his boss gives him a very important project which will entail at least two hours' work and which has to be completed that day. However, John wants to leave on time because he is planning to meet his fiancée after work to go and choose an engagement ring.

Response 1
John feels really angry and starts the work with a bad grace. At 5pm he explodes with frustration and anger, upsets his cold coffee all over his desk and storms into the boss's office saying he is sick of the job and how thoughtless his boss is. He meets his fiancée as arranged but the evening is spoilt as he feels guilty about his angry outburst.

Aggressive □   Assertive □   Passive □

Response 2
John is really angry inside, but wants to please his boss, so he phones his fiancée, saying he will be late. He then stays and works on the project, muttering under his breath, 'How dare he do this to me?' He suffers in silence and by the time he has completed the work he is so tired, angry and irritable that the evening with his fiancée is spoilt.

Aggressive □   Assertive □   Passive □

Response 3
John explains to his boss that today he really would like to leave on time, because he has promised his fiancée that they would buy the engagement ring that evening. He offers to come in early the next morning to do the work if it really is so urgent.

Aggressive □   Assertive □   Passive □

SCENARIO B
In a crowded train carriage which is designated 'quiet' and which has clear signs marked 'No mobile phones', a passenger sitting opposite Jenny is talking loudly and at length into his mobile. Jenny has a headache and wants to rest.

Response 1
Jenny gets up and leaves the carriage.
  Aggressive ☐   Assertive ☐   Passive ☐

Response 2
Jenny points to the 'No mobile phones' notice and says, 'This is a quiet carriage. Please would you mind moving to another one where mobiles are permitted?'
  Aggressive ☐   Assertive ☐   Passive ☐

Response 3
Jenny sighs angrily and dramatically, then says to the man, 'Don't you care about other people? I have a terrible headache and your antisocial behaviour is just making it worse. Why can't you think about anything except what you want to do? Switch that phone off and stop plaguing me or find another carriage!'
  Aggressive ☐   Assertive ☐   Passive ☐

SCENARIO C
In a packed Royal Albert Hall, the people in front of Mr Smith and his wife, who is in a wheelchair, keep standing up to clap and cheer the singers, thus obliterating the view for Mrs Smith.

Response 1
Mr and Mrs Smith suffer in silence and say nothing.
  Aggressive ☐   Assertive ☐   Passive ☐

Response 2
Mr Smith pokes the people in front of them and snaps, 'Have you no consideration for those less fortunate than yourselves?

Have you no respect for others? I'm going to complain to the management!'

Aggressive □   Assertive □   Passive □

Response 3

Mr Smith gently taps the people in front on the shoulder and says, 'Excuse me, would you mind sitting down, please, as my wife is in a wheelchair and she can't see when you stand up? Thank you.'

Aggressive □   Assertive □   Passive □

ACTIVITY

Can you think of a recent example of passive behaviour in your own life? If so, try writing down three responses – aggressive, assertive and passive – as in the scenarios above. How might you have responded differently in the situation in which you found yourself?

REFLECTION

Think about some of the ideas presented in this chapter. Reflecting on the truth that you are made in God's image, consider how you would like to be different from the way you are at the moment. Then, if you can, pray the following prayer.

PRAYER

Loving heavenly Father, I would like to be different, but I know I am a work in progress! Please fill me with Your Holy Spirit, for I know that He is the One who can give me the power to change. Lord, help me to become more like Jesus, growing in the ability to be assertive. Thank You, Lord. Amen.

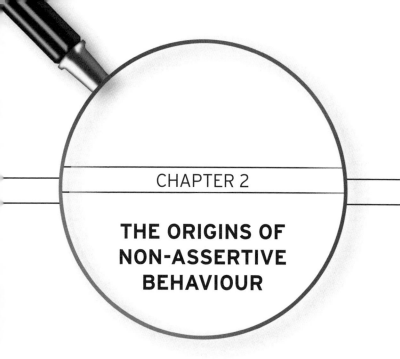

CHAPTER 2

THE ORIGINS OF NON-ASSERTIVE BEHAVIOUR

Be careful what you think, because your thoughts run your life.

(Proverbs 4.23, NCV)

Look back at the three scenarios in the activity at the end of the last chapter. If you identified your own response as passive in more than one instance, you are not an assertive person and over the years, you may have turned into a people-pleaser, to the extent that you always put other people's needs before your own, never say no to a request, and by now may even have forgotten how to express your own needs and desires.

When we are people-pleasers, our thoughts, feelings, behaviour and spiritual lives are all affected. All human beings are born with instinctive longings for love, approval and acceptance. Ideally, these longings are met in our earliest years by the positive, focused attention we receive from our parents – or, in the absence of parents, our primary caregivers – so that we know that we are loved, valued and accepted unconditionally. We realise that our parents' love for us is not dependent on how we behave, or on how clever, pretty or creative we are. Children so blessed grow up with healthy self-esteem, or what we sometimes call a strong sense of self-worth. They tend not to become people-pleasers.

Unfortunately, no parents are perfect. Consequently, many of us, somewhere along the line, begin to equate our self-worth – our acceptance of ourselves – with our parents' *approval*. We may even believe that we aren't loved if we don't do what our parents want, and we are loved when we are 'nice', 'good' or 'obedient'. Can you see where we're going? As we develop into adolescents and adults, we may try to find our self-worth by gaining other people's approval or love or respect … by doing what *they* want. Some of us may have developed a deep-seated fear of rejection, feeling afraid of losing love or approval if we don't do what people want and, slowly but surely, we turn into people-pleasers, giving in to others' demands or requests, however unreasonable or inappropriate these may be, whilst simultaneously making huge demands on, and being very critical of, ourselves.

> Jane grew up with a very dominant, critical and controlling mother and, from an early age, learnt that by always pleasing her mother fewer harsh words were thrown at her. Marriage and children of her own brought further problems. Jane was so used to pleasing her mother that she still allowed her to dominate to such an extent that she even dictated what clothes Jane and the children wore, and how Jane lived her life. (If Jane didn't comply, her mother said she didn't love her.) Unsurprisingly, Jane became very depressed for years,

and it was only through counselling, where she learnt assertiveness skills, that she began to break free of her mother's domination and the depression lifted.

To small children, adults – especially parents and teachers (authority figures) – can seem all-powerful. A parent's anger can be very, very frightening to a young child, and most small children will do anything to avoid it. So they learn very quickly that to avoid anger or punishment, they must be 'nice' or 'good'. Being 'nice' to others or being 'good' results in praise; not being so results in displeasure from the authority figure. The lesson is rapidly absorbed: 'If I am "not nice" or "bad" (ie if I break family rules or challenge parental authority) I get an angry response, or even punishment, and I feel bad about myself – so I must be a bad person. If I am "nice" or "good" I get praise and I feel good about myself – therefore, I must be a good person.' The child's subconscious logic then goes a step further: 'If I am nice/good the things I don't like – anger and discipline – don't happen, so *if I keep on being nice it will stop bad things happening to me and people will like me and approve of me.*'

Sometimes the thinking goes even further than this. Children can assume a feeling of omnipotence, believing that they are actually in control of everything and that they can therefore fend off bad consequences, consequences which are not actually within the child's power. Sometimes we can unwittingly carry this belief into our adult lives, so when as adults we are stressed and life feels overwhelming, we may try to take control again by working harder at being 'good' or 'nice' in order to influence the outcome of whatever situation is giving rise to the stress we're under – relationships, illness, accident and so on.

Similarly, some adults carry forward their childhood guilt that traumatic events might never have happened if they had been 'nicer' or 'better' children. We have all read, for example, of children who suffer for years after a parental split because they believe that their 'naughtiness' was responsible for the break-up of the relationship between their parents. Other traumatic events such as a death in the family can trigger similar guilt.

> Charlie's younger brother died when Charlie was five, but because his parents never talked about it, Charlie believed that his brother's death had somehow been his fault. He grew up trying to be 'good' to compensate for his brother's death, always motivated by a need to please his parents, because he didn't want to cause them any more grief.

Such beliefs are deeply embedded in the consciousness of many people-pleasers and we don't realise their origins. Because we are unaware of their roots in our early childhood experiences it comes as a shock to recognise that they have infused our sense of self. We may believe that being 'nice' and pleasing other people can protect us from life's difficulties and from being disapproved of or rejected. This will put a heavy burden on us, both in our thinking and our behaviour. But God didn't make us to strive to be 'nice' to everyone all the time and He doesn't expect it of us!

One difficulty is that in some families – especially Christian families – we are taught that 'niceness' is synonymous with being unselfish, and unselfishness is elevated above all other virtues. For example:

> It's Matthew's fourth birthday and he's been given another engine for his much-loved *Thomas the Tank Engine* train set, which is shared

with his little brother, Josh, who's two. Josh wants to play with the new engine and kicks up such a fuss that Matthew, somewhat reluctantly, hands it over, allowing Josh to play with it. Matthew is then praised by his parents for being unselfish – for 'being nice' to Josh. However, in actual fact, in that situation, it might be more important for Josh to learn about boundaries and birthdays and other people's possessions. Meanwhile poor little Matthew has 'learned' that he has to be 'unselfish' and 'nice' even if it means giving up things that are legitimately his, whilst Josh has learned the very dubious lesson that if he makes enough fuss he'll get whatever he wants.

Many of us who were brought up in fairly strict Christian homes will recognise the kind of scenario described above – especially if we had younger siblings. This can carry over into adult life; we can think that other people's needs are *always* more important or more pressing than our own, and what we don't realise is that there is a significant difference between exercising enlightened self-interest and being selfish.

PEOPLE-PLEASING BEHAVIOUR IS LEARNED BEHAVIOUR

From their earliest moments, children come to have a sense of who they are (their 'identity') through their parents. So they learn to associate smiling faces and approving sounds with security and love. When parents offer their children unconditional love, those children get the message that they are loved come what may, irrespective of what they do, even if sometimes their behaviour is unacceptable: 'I love you very much but I don't like what you just did.' This unconditional love of parents mirrors the love that God offers to us all.

If, on the other hand, children learn that parental love and approval is conditional, ie that it can be withdrawn, but may be earned by being 'good' or 'nice' and pleasing their parents, they will try hard to please constantly because they fear rejection and abandonment if they don't. Children have a very immature understanding of who they are and believe that who they are is the same as what they do, so they make untrue assumptions: 'When I do something "bad" *I* am bad; if I do something "good/nice", *I* am "good/nice".' Sometimes parents unwittingly reinforce this idea by saying to children who have misbehaved, 'You are naughty!' instead of 'That was a naughty thing to do!' So children who are not loved unconditionally feel that they have to please others in order to win acceptance, approval and love – and that feeling can carry over into adult life. Let's look at some of the areas where people-pleasers get things wrong.

AREAS AFFECTED WHEN WE ARE PEOPLE-PLEASERS

OUR SPIRITUAL LIVES

Throughout the Bible, from beginning to end, we find the theme of God wanting relationship with human beings, and of His finding ways to reach out to us in order to make that relationship possible. As human beings we are made in God's image, and therefore we need relationships – with God and with one another. God longs for us to know that we are *unconditionally* loved and valued by Him, as individuals, whatever our gender, race, colour, gifts, abilities … and failings. He loves me! He loves you – just as you are. As Philip Yancey so succinctly puts it, 'There is nothing you or I can do to make God love us any more; there is nothing you or I can do to make God love us any less.'[1]

God loves us, each one of us, and wants to pour His love and acceptance into our innermost beings. It is ultimately only from God's unconditional love that we derive our sense of our own value, our self-worth. But even those of us who have been Christians for years sometimes find it hard to accept that, and go on looking for love and acceptance outside of God. Some of us try to find our sense of worth by people-pleasing. It may seem to work for a while, but it takes so much time and energy, because we can never say no, never let up; we always have to meet other people's needs, or else they may disapprove of us, or reject us, or stop loving us. We're like hamsters on a wheel in a cage, going round and round and round, and never getting anywhere.

In the Old Testament, God says to Jeremiah, 'My people have committed two sins: They have forsaken me, the spring of living water, and have dug their own cisterns, broken cisterns that cannot hold water' (Jer. 2:13). People-pleasers do just that: having failed to find self-worth in God – the everlasting source of what Jesus later also called 'living water' (John 4:10) – we effectively dig our 'own cisterns' only to find these 'containers' don't hold water, and have to be constantly 'filled up' – by people-pleasing.

OUR THINKING

People-pleasers' thought patterns, too, are often skewed and faulty. At root we are driven by the idea that we have to behave in such a way that everyone will like and approve of us. We are motivated by our need for universal acceptance, basing our sense of identity and self-worth on how much we do for other people, whose needs *must* be put before our own. At the same time, we are very critical of our 'performance' in the area of helping other people, making ridiculous demands on ourselves and being critical of anything less than perfection.

What's the solution? We have already seen that *assertiveness is a skill that can be learnt*! Flawed and rigid thought patterns result in flawed behaviour patterns, so before we can change our behaviour and start saying no, we have to learn to change our thought patterns. Just as we thought our way into being non-assertive so we can think our way out of it, by finding alternative thoughts and challenging our beliefs.

OUR FEELINGS

People-pleasers, consciously or unconsciously, avoid uncomfortable emotions because they are too frightening for them to handle. They tend to anticipate (or, more often, imagine) situations of conflict and confrontation where such emotions may be unleashed, and then avoid those situations. They are driven by the need to protect themselves from such situations because they can't handle the emotions involved, and fear the rejection or disapproval of others that may be expressed in the interchanges that conflict and confrontation inevitably bring.

However, by avoiding difficult situations, people-pleasers never learn to *handle conflict or manage anger*. One result of this can be that they hand over control to people who get what they want by intimidation and manipulation. Avoiding feared situations only maintains or increases our level of fear, but we can learn how to handle and manage anger and conflict, and thus overcome our fear of them.

Another 'emotion to be avoided' by people-pleasers is guilt. We all understand the expression, 'I felt guilty' but guilt can plague people-pleasers; so, in order to avoid feeling guilty, they keep

THE ORIGINS OF NON-ASSERTIVE BEHAVIOUR

working at doing things for others – then they won't feel guilty about not meeting other people's needs or requests or demands.

What exactly is guilt? Guilt is a state of internal condemnation, arising from an overstrict, critical conscience, but the things we feel guilty about need not necessarily have moral overtones at all. For example, if we were brought up in a home where we were reprimanded whenever we closed a door noisily (even accidentally), then in adult life, whenever we close a door noisily, our conscience will prick us: 'You slammed that door – naughty!' God does not make us feel guilty – the Holy Spirit does not condemn us; yes, He 'convicts' us of sin (real guilt), but that's not the same as inducing false guilt. When God the Holy Spirit shows us something is wrong, He will also show us, either from the Bible or from trusted Christians, what to do about it. With false guilt there is no way out, no way to get rid of it; we just go round and round in circles listening to our conscience saying, 'You should/ shouldn't have done that!' It's a totally useless and futile emotion. Those of us who have oversensitive consciences – often a result of our upbringing – will condemn ourselves for things that God doesn't condemn us for. This is what Paul refers to, in a slightly different context, as a 'weak' conscience (1 Cor. 8).

Mary's elderly neighbour, Bob, fell over and broke his leg. He had no family, and his other neighbours were also elderly so Mary and her husband found themselves visiting him in hospital, keeping an eye on his house and garden, doing his washing and so on. When discharged from hospital Bob wasn't well enough to cope alone, so at first Mary would go in three times daily. Slowly Bob got more mobile, but still wanted Mary to go in as frequently as she had been doing – and when Mary didn't, he showed his displeasure.

Mary found this hard to cope with; she felt she was letting Bob down. Like many people-pleasers she 'felt guilty' when Bob was upset because of her 'failures', finding it hard to handle what seemed to her a conflict situation. Bob was, consciously or unconsciously, trying to manipulate Mary by playing on her sense of guilt. Mary – very busy anyway – was wearing herself out. She found herself repeatedly thinking, 'I ought to visit Bob,' and feeling both guilty that she didn't do so and resentful that Bob expected her to. Finally she asked herself, 'Why ought I to go?' and recognised that she couldn't allow Bob to manipulate her.

OUR BEHAVIOUR PATTERNS

Looking for self-acceptance outside of God's unconditional love, flawed thinking and avoidance of uncomfortable emotions can all lead to unhelpful behaviour patterns in the people-pleaser. We take care of others' needs at the expense of our own (and sometimes those of our immediate family); we rarely say no, overcommit to doing too much (often for too many other people), and then find ourselves, for example, doing our own ironing in the small hours, depriving ourselves of sleep with all the negative consequences that brings for us and those for whom we are primarily responsible! If this becomes a habitual pattern, it eventually leads to 'burnout'. (Chris O moved to a new church with her husband when he was ordained, then caught herself reading of a need in her previous church and automatically thinking, 'I could do that', before realising that it was no longer her responsibility. People-pleasers tend to think that if there is a need they can meet, then they *have* to meet it.)

We can be driven by the need for approval – we *have to* help with the washing-up at every church function because otherwise what sort of Christian will people think we are? Or we *have to* run a stall at the school Christmas Fair because people know we're a Christian so we *must* be seen to be doing our bit in the wider community, as well as at church. This kind of thinking can even become addictive.

Chris O finally recognised this when one of her adult daughters bought her a book, handing it to her with the words, 'Don't be offended, Mum, but I saw this and thought it might help you.' The book was called *Approval Addiction* and, as Chris read it, she realised that she did indeed have a problem in that area – but her daughter had recognised it before she did.

However, it is possible to learn how to break such behaviour patterns, first by changing our thought patterns and then by thinking before we commit to any action.

Of course, not every people-pleaser will have problems in all these areas, and many will recognise themselves more clearly in one area than another. But the root cause of flawed thinking, avoidance of uncomfortable emotions, or self-destructive behaviour patterns, is always a faulty spiritual foundation – trying to find our sense of self-worth other than in God.

Lack of assertiveness is just the symptom of an underlying 'sickness' – yes, assertiveness is a skill that can be learnt and a useful tool, but one that is easier to use if the root causes of the 'sickness' are diagnosed and dealt with. The *key* issue at the heart of the quest for assertiveness is finding our sense of identity in God. Ultimately the only thing I can say about who I am is that I am loved by God. That is why I exist. Loving and uplifting relationships with family and friends are the icing on the cake of life – but even if I were to lose all my friends and family and everybody despised me, *God would still love me.* This is the only thing in our lives that will never change, and therefore the only thing on which we may legitimately and confidently pin our hope. It is the only thing from which we may safely gain our sense of identity and self-worth.

(Ingrid Fearnehough in a letter to Chris O.)

ACTIVITY

Dig out some old photos of yourself as a child. Try to remember what it was like in your home/school/situation at that age. Can you see where seeds were sown for you to become a people-pleaser? Ask God to reveal to you anything He wants to show you.

REFLECTION

Think about what God has shown you as you have read this chapter and looked at the photos of yourself growing up. Consciously acknowledge these and then think about how, with God's help, you can begin to break free from old patterns of thinking and acting. Consider talking these matters through with someone you trust so that you can be accountable to them as you implement changes.

PRAYER

Loving Father, thank You that You know all about me, and love me unconditionally, just as I am, right now! You understand the particular combination of temperament, personality and childhood circumstances that have contributed to my becoming a people-pleaser. I bring all this to You now and ask that You will help me to break free. I can't do it by myself. I can't do it overnight. Help me to do it in Your way and in Your time. Thank You, Lord. Amen.

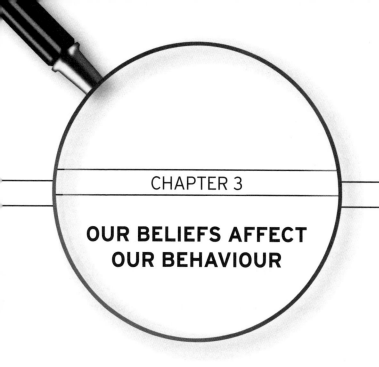

CHAPTER 3

OUR BELIEFS AFFECT OUR BEHAVIOUR

There is only one cause of unhappiness: the false beliefs you have in your head, beliefs so ... commonly held, that it never occurs to you to question them.

(Anthony de Mello)

We have just considered some ways in which our skewed and rigid thinking can influence the way we act. In a similar way, flawed beliefs – about life, other people, ourselves and God – can affect our behaviour and our ability to be assertive.

FLAWED BELIEFS ABOUT LIFE

We noted earlier that children quickly learn that being 'nice' or 'good' can protect them from adult anger and punishment, and how sometimes childish logic takes this a step further so that they come to believe that by being 'nice' they can prevent any bad things happening to them.

The 'belief package' goes something like this:

If I'm 'nice' or 'good' and do what people want.
↓
They will like me.
↓
Then I won't get hurt and rejected.
↓
Because if I'm rejected I'm obviously a bad person and will feel worthless.

These skewed beliefs, and the reasoning that results from them, can take us spiralling downwards into depression. We can then feel the urge to try even harder to please, and the vicious cycle continues. There is nothing wrong with the actual reasoning above, which is perfectly logical. *But the premise on which that belief is based* (that life is fair and people get what they deserve) *is false.*

The reality is this:
- Life *isn't* fair. We live in a fallen, broken world and it's only by God's grace that things aren't irretrievably bad.
- Bad things *do* happen to good people!
- Niceness doesn't protect us from trauma.
The solution:
Modify your beliefs. Accept that:
- Life isn't fair – however much we want to believe it should be.

- It's OK not to be nice all the time.
- It's OK not to please other people all the time.
- People will reject us at times, but that doesn't mean we are 'bad' people.

FLAWED BELIEFS ABOUT OTHER PEOPLE

- Others must always come first.
- It is my responsibility to do something when others are upset.
- If other people dislike me, it must be my fault.

These are probably the most common faulty beliefs about other people. They may have been family rules when the people-pleaser was growing up, and they can engender a belief that the needs and demands of other people are *always* of paramount importance. This can mean that we are driven to satisfy other people's demands and meet their needs at the expense of our own. We can find ourselves putting 'other people' before God. We fear people more than we fear God. In other words, we are more concerned about what other people think than about what God thinks.

FLAWED BELIEFS ABOUT OURSELVES

These can include:

- My value depends on what I do.
- I am only worthy of others' love if I do things for them.
- My role in life is to make everyone else happy.
- If I upset people by being honest, I'm a terrible person.

The problem with beliefs like these is that they can lead to other erroneous beliefs; for example, that there is no value in doing things that will be of benefit *to ourselves*, such as going for a walk on a lovely day, visiting the gym, taking a nap, soaking in the bath or going out for coffee. The danger is that the belief 'My value depends on what I do' becomes self-defeating because we can't give ourselves permission to unwind and relax – which is vital for our overall wellbeing.

Clues to such erroneous beliefs about ourselves can be found in certain phrases and expressions, such as:

• Oh, I never stop.

This telltale phrase is a bit of a giveaway! It may be said with a sigh or in a tone of resignation, indicating 'the martyr' – or with a sense of pride, indicating 'the competitor' – 'I intend to win the "Does the Most for Other People" trophy'.

With this kind of belief driving us, it's very easy to become a slave to other people's wishes, and people-pleasers are often perfectionists, never satisfied with what has been accomplished. We never give ourselves a pat on the back, or hear God say: 'Well done, good and faithful servant.'

• It's always better to give than to receive.

When we are driven by this belief, we tend to give constantly to others and deny them the pleasure – and blessing – of giving to us in return. It's hard to acknowledge that this is in fact manipulative, and rejecting, behaviour. Sometimes we may want to 'buy' the relationship (possibly in order to take control) and at other times we may subconsciously want others to feel inferior to us, so we never let them do anything for us.

RESULTS OF THESE FLAWED BELIEFS - RELATIONSHIPS ARE AFFECTED

- People may feel inadequate in their relationships with us because what *they* want to give to us is never accepted.
- People may end up feeling guilty in the relationship because they're never permitted to do anything for us.
- People may feel beholden, indebted and duty-bound to us.

FLAWED BELIEF ABOUT GOD:

- I must always strive to please God.

Unfortunately, this one can be reinforced by the teaching in some churches – especially, evangelical ones – so it may take a while to recognise that it is, in fact, erroneous. God does *not* want us to 'burn out' for Him! He does not wish to see us in a constant state of tension and anxiety about whether or not we are pleasing Him and 'doing enough' for Him. Jesus always pleased God: He was the beloved Son, with whom God was 'well pleased' (Luke 3:22), yet we never read of Him struggling and striving to achieve and accomplish in order to please His Father. God's love flowed through Jesus and out to others in an unpressurised way. He wasn't tense, harassed and anxious, always rushing to the next thing on His list!

Some Christians, especially people-pleasers, approach God in a similar way to that in which they approach other people – with a desire to please Him and to do what He wants. In one sense, there is nothing wrong with this: every Christian's goal is to live in a way that pleases God. But when we look more closely, we see that, as with people-pleasing, there is a sometimes unrecognised 'hidden agenda'. What is driving this behaviour? People-pleasers

37

strive to please God *because, very often, either knowingly or unknowingly, they want God to give them something* (acceptance, a sense of worth, an answer to prayer), or believe that by 'doing things' for Him, God will love them more, and therefore be more inclined to answer their prayer. This is actually trying to manipulate God. They 'surrender' to God not as a genuine response to His love but *so that* He may bestow His favours on them. They are trying to wangle things out of God, to bargain with Him: 'I'll do this for You if You'll do that for me.' This is the wrong way round! Submitting to God's love is a *response* to His great love for us, demonstrated most obviously in the cross; it is not a device to get things from Him. Let's remind ourselves once again of Philip Yancey's words in his book, *What's so Amazing about Grace?*: 'There is nothing you or I can do to make God love us any more; there is nothing you or I can do to make God love us any less.'[1]

Of course, if we strive to please God in the expectation that He will then do what we want, and our prayers aren't answered in the way we wish, we are setting ourselves up for disappointment and frustration – with God, not other people, as the focus.

'NICE' PEOPLE

Glance back once more to the three scenarios at the end of Chapter 1. If you identified your own response as *passive* in more than one instance, you are almost certainly viewed by those who know you as a very 'nice' person – and that's probably how you would like to think of yourself. But, for all of us who would answer in the same way: all too often the effect on our emotional and physical health is enormous. In the effort to keep everyone else happy, we rarely feel comfortable with ourselves. In other words, 'niceness' has a hidden cost.

This hidden cost may be a serious psychological problem. People pleasing can develop into a compulsive behaviour pattern where the need to please other people controls us, and we become addicted to their approval. This sort of non-assertive behaviour pattern can have several manifestations. For example:

- *Our lives feel out of control* as a result of the demands on us created by this addictive/compulsive need, and we may end up with debilitating stress and exhaustion.
- *Our emotional tuning becomes oversensitised* so that it goes off like an alarm whenever we believe that others want or expect something from us. We listen to this 'alarm', rather than to the inner voice reminding us of our own needs, and trying to protect us from burnout.
- *Our self-esteem gets tied into pleasing others* and meeting their needs, in order to gain love and a sense of self-worth. As a result, we invariably find ourselves overwhelmed by insecurities, doubts and fears, because our sense of self-worth is still rooted in other people's approval; we haven't truly found our security in God.
- *Our identity is affected* because it is derived from that image of being a 'nice' person, and we expend so much energy in maintaining that image that in the end, we may not know who we are – we can't separate our real self from the 'nice' persona we have adopted. This inevitably affects our relationship with God because, spiritually, something within us dies.

To sum up: we pay a high price when we are driven by a need to gain the approval of others by 'being nice'. It's possible to end up pleasing no one and not looking after ourselves into the bargain. Yes, Jesus said, 'Love your neighbour as yourself' (Mark 12:31) – but so many 'nice' people don't really love themselves, so how can they even begin to love their neighbours?

SELFISH VERSUS SELFLESS

Being either selfish or selfless is often seen as an all-or-nothing or black-and-white choice. People think they must be either utterly selfless, always putting others' needs and welfare before their own (the People-Pleaser), *or* completely selfish to the point of trampling on and discarding others for their own gain, by putting their own needs and desires first and foremost (the Arrogant Abuser).

God doesn't want or expect us to live as totally 'selfless' people. He says we are important. The danger is that when we always put others' needs before our own we become less than effective for God's kingdom and run the risk of not being fulfilled at all. Why? Because if we set out to be 'totally selfless' we run a huge risk of harbouring deep resentments. That is the cost – the pay-off. The gain may be (genuine or apparent) acceptance by other people, but the price we pay is huge, and the result is that others suffer because we are not living in the fullness that Christ has for us.

If we are uncertain about how 'Christian' it is *not* to be utterly selfless, we can turn to the Bible. In Philippians Paul says this: 'Each of you should look not only to your own interests, but also to the interests of others' (Phil. 2:4). Notice that he doesn't say we *shouldn't* look to our own interests, but that we should *not only* look to those, but *also* to those of others.

Jesus, the ultimate example of selflessness, was assertive

in the best possible way. Although He said '… even the Son of Man did not come to be served but to serve' (Mark 10:45), He was not at everyone's beck and call all the time; He spent time alone with His Father, and took His disciples off for times of quiet and solitude. He said, 'Love your neighbour as you love yourself' (Mark 12:31, NCV) … yes, as you love *yourself*. We may choose to burn ourselves out and sacrifice our own needs for the sake of keeping the peace and being 'nice', but this doesn't necessarily mean that we are being unselfish; in fact, it's more likely that we're pushing the self-destruct button. We may find ourselves very successful at making other people happy, but feel miserable failures inside. So we may need to redefine our interpretation of the words 'selfishness' and 'nice'.

If 'being nice', ie doing what other people want or expect of us, is our highest aspiration because we believe that 'being nice' equates to being a loving Christian person, then 'niceness' becomes not life-transforming, but merely self-enhancing. Following Jesus is *not* about being 'nice' people who don't like to give offence. If we are afraid of offending people, we forget that the gospel – with its message that we can do nothing to save ourselves and that we all need God – is offensive. As Paul reminds us (1 Cor. 1:23) the cross was a 'stumbling-block' (literally, 'scandalous') to Jews and folly to Greeks – the two peoples making up the civilised world in the days of the Early Church. If our chief aim is to avoid giving offence because, deep down, we fear confrontation or rejection, then there will be little passion or effectiveness to our Christian witness, and the radical nature of the good news of Jesus is lost.

If we cannot acknowledge and express negative emotions we are not being real and authentic Christians. Jesus said, 'Blessed are the peacemakers' (Matt. 5:9), but He neither subscribed to the 'peace at any price' concept nor avoided conflict with the religious establishment. Conflict avoidance is not an ingredient of successful relationships. We need to recognise that uncomfortable feelings are inevitable at times; the challenge is learning to deal with them effectively. When conflict is not avoided, but handled constructively with appropriately expressed feelings, our relationships are in better working order.

Perhaps you've read this far and recognise yourself in many of the statements, but you have some questions. 'This is all very well,' you may think, 'but what about Jesus' words about denying myself, about taking up my cross daily and following Him? Isn't that what I'm trying to do?'

These are valid questions, but it has to be said that many preachers may have used these words of Jesus manipulatively – and sometimes out of context. Inducing guilt is a tactic not confined to secular organisations. Some of us may have been brought up in churches where 'burning out for God' was held up as something desirable – a goal to aim for, although the fallout for the families of those who 'burn out for God' was certainly neither desirable nor in any way glorifying to God.

Let's look at Jesus; He lived for others, He 'went around doing good' (Acts 10:38); He was compassionate and loving. He gave Himself in teaching and healing. Sometimes He challenged the religious establishment, and sometimes He was angry – for example, when the disciples tried to prevent small children being brought to Him for blessing. He attended weddings and dinner parties – He lived! He was clearly what today we would call a 'busy' person. But nowhere in the Gospels is there any suggestion that Jesus ever appeared harassed or overwrought or short-tempered from lack of sleep.

Why? Because Jesus' beliefs were not flawed; He was assertive in the best possible way. He achieved the perfect balance between work and rest, between listening to God and listening to others. He rose before it was light to spend time with God, or took His disciples away from the crowds to rest and relax together. His goals were set and He moved towards them unflinchingly, but not to the exclusion of other people and their physical, emotional and spiritual needs. He was single-minded, but not blinkered. *Most significantly, Jesus had no need of others' approval because He knew, deep in His innermost being, that He was God's beloved Son – and that was enough.*

So some of us 'nice' Christian people-pleasers have got it skewed. There may be a number of reasons for this. We may truly believe that dying to self means that God wants us to wear ourselves out for others; we may have accepted 'in our heads' that we are loved and valued unconditionally by God, but for some reason we have never been able to allow that knowledge to take root in our hearts and flood our souls with a deep sense of belonging and worth – so we may still be looking for acceptance and approval from other people by trying to please them. We may even be trying to gain *God's* approval by doing things for others. Let's listen to Philip Yancey once again: *There is nothing you or I can do to make God love us any more; there is nothing you or I can do to make God love us any less.'*[2]

Jesus' own words highlight another significant key to His life and ministry. In John's Gospel, we read: 'I tell you the truth, the Son can do nothing by himself; he can do only what he sees his Father doing, because whatever the Father does the Son also does' (John 5:19). Later, Jesus says, 'I do nothing on my own but speak just what the Father has taught me' (John 8:28), and in John 10:37 He says, 'Do not believe me unless I do what my Father does.' Jesus' life of 'doing good' sprang not from a frantic desire to gain approval or significance or self-worth, but from living in relationship with His Father and sharing His Father's ministry, joining with what God His Father was already doing. Mission originates with God! As we recognise that our self-worth ultimately comes from knowing that we are deeply loved by, and of immense value to, God, then instead of being driven by our need for others' approval, we can find ourselves working *with* God in our daily lives.

ACTIVITY

'My needs are not important.'

To what extent am I driven by this belief?

Scale the intensity of this belief 1–10 (10 being high) when faced with:

- Family demands
- Work demands
- Friends' demands

How does this belief affect my behaviour with these groups of people?

REFLECTION

Read and reflect on Paul's words in Ephesians 2:10: 'For we are God's workmanship, created in Christ Jesus to do good works, which God prepared in advance for us to do.' You may find it helpful to compare different versions (such as NCV, NKJV, *The Message*). You may also find it helpful to write the verse out and stick it on your fridge, or in your Bible, or in your diary – somewhere where it can act as a reminder to you to be led, not driven.

To help you reflect, try using the following:

- What does the word 'workmanship' suggest? What does it mean for you personally to be 'God's workmanship'? What practical implications does this have for your daily life?
- How has a flawed belief about yourself, others or God affected your ability to be the person God wants you to be?
- How do the words 'good works … prepared in advance' make you feel?

PRAYER
Dear Father, please open my eyes to what You want to show me. Please help me to change my beliefs where You want them to change. Lord, as You put Your finger on these things, I know You are more than willing to give me the power to change. Help me to become the person You want me to be. Thank You, gracious Lord, that You have prepared good works for me to do. Amen.

CHAPTER 4

UNHELPFUL THOUGHT PATTERNS

… there is nothing either good or bad, but thinking makes it so …
(Shakespeare: *Hamlet*, Act 2: Scene 2)

'To paraphrase Shakespeare: "There is nothing either good or bad but *rigid, dogmatic* thinking makes it so."' The words in italics were inserted into the Shakespeare quotation by Dr Windy Dryden in *Assertiveness Step by Step*[1], to make the point that inflexible thinking can prevent us from growing in assertiveness.

DISTORTED THINKING

The way in which we apply our beliefs has a powerful effect on our thinking. When we feel uncomfortable, stressed or depressed, our thinking becomes even more exaggerated and distorted.

Below are some common distortions of our thinking:

- *All or nothing*: We think in absolutes: good or bad; black or white, with no grey areas or middle ground, eg 'I'll be seen as a bad person if I don't say I'll do it.'
- *Catastrophising*: We exaggerate or overdramatise, believing the worst will happen, eg 'If I don't babysit for them this evening, it will be awful!'
- *Jumping to conclusions*: We make negative predictions without evidence or facts, eg 'I *must* take on the leadership role; otherwise the group will become non-viable.'
- *Personalising*: We take responsibility for everything that goes wrong, feeling we are to blame, eg 'If I don't say yes to helping him with his revision and he fails, it will be my fault.'
- *Emotional reasoning*: We evaluate situations according to how we feel, eg 'I'm too frightened to say no, because I know he'll shout at me.'

RIGID THINKING

People-pleasers are driven by the words *should, ought, must* and *have to*, which are constantly in our heads, and often on our lips too. Listen to a people-pleaser's conversation and notice how often one of the words above crops up! They are part and parcel of a set of self-imposed rules and expectations about how we – and other people – behave. These rigid thinking patterns prevent us from becoming assertive. Dr Karen Horney[2] talks about 'the *tyranny* of the should' to convey the ability of that little word to enslave us with self-imposed rules. Another name for the power of the words *should, ought, must, have to* is the 'Disease of the Oughteries'! The punning label highlights a very real problem:

if we are enslaved by *should, ought, must*, we are indeed dis-eased – uncomfortable with ourselves, never satisfied that we're doing enough to make ourselves valued and appreciated.

Unfortunately, when these *shoulds, oughts, musts* and *have tos* diffuse into our thought patterns, they disturb our emotions and destroy our capacity for feeling satisfied, fulfilled and at peace. These little words put constant pressure on us to attain our internal (and self-imposed) standards:

- I *mustn't* let anyone down, because if I do, I'm not loving them as I should.
- I *ought to* visit my elderly neighbour, even though I'm exhausted.
- I *have* to make that cake for church even though I'm unwell, because I promised the vicar's wife …
- I really *should* phone Mrs Jones to find out how she is.

When we don't match up to our self-imposed internal standards, we feel guilty and angry with ourselves, and can become very self-critical. This often leads to discouragement and depression. Sometimes we then go even further and start imposing these standards on other people:

- My husband *ought* to have been home for dinner.
- My grown-up daughter *shouldn't* have left me to hang out her washing.
- My friend *must* stop giving me advice.
- My son *has to* learn to respect other people's property.

In doing this we set ourselves up for frustration and anger when the people on whom we've (silently) imposed our standards don't come up to our expectations – and we can't force them to. We end up feeling disappointed, unappreciated – and worthless. What it boils down to is that we think others *should* behave in particular ways, so that we may feel good about ourselves. We can therefore develop unrealistic (and of course, unexpressed) demands of other people.

TEN COMMANDMENTS FOR OTHER PEOPLE

1   Other people *should* always like me because of all the things I do for them.
2. Other people *must* never reject me because I always do what they want.
3. Other people *ought to* appreciate me because I always keep the peace.
4. Other people *should* be caring towards me because I am caring towards them.
5. Other people *shouldn't* be angry with me because I never show anger to them.
6. Other people *ought* not to hurt me because I'm never unkind to them.
7. Other people *shouldn't* criticise me because I do my best to please them.
8. Other people *should* always like me because I put myself out for them.
9. Other people *ought* to love me because I am always a 'nice' person.
10. Other people *ought* always to thank me when I do anything for them.

As you read the list, even if you now recognise that you have people-pleasing tendencies, you may think, 'That's a bit of an exaggeration; I'm sure I don't do that.' Chris O thought that too, until she got to the last one and realised how hurt she can feel when people don't acknowledge or thank her for something!

CHANGING OUR THOUGHT PATTERNS

We can change our flawed and rigid thought patterns and doing so will, in turn, influence our behaviour patterns. For example, we can practise changing the *should* rules into statements reflecting our desires or preferences. So we turn a command or demand into a request or suggestion: instead of 'I *must*', 'I *have to*', 'I *ought to*' or 'I *really should*', we say to ourselves, ' I *wish*', 'I'd *like to*', 'I'd *rather*', I *would prefer*'. So, for example: 'I *ought to* visit my elderly neighbour' might become 'I *would like to* visit my elderly neighbour', and 'My teenager *ought* to tidy her bedroom every week' might become 'I *would prefer* it if my teenager tidied her bedroom every week.'

Using this kind of strategy has two outcomes. Firstly, it takes the pressure off us and secondly, it's much more realistic, especially when we're dealing with our own expectations of others. 'I *wish* other people would like me' is more realistic than 'Other people *should* like me', since we cannot control what others choose and feel. Expressing our thoughts as requests or desires suggests (quite correctly) that others have the freedom to make choices, even though those choices may not be what we would like. So, 'I *wish* my family wouldn't reject me every time I don't live up to their expectations' is a much more realistic statement than 'My family *shouldn't* reject me every time I fail an exam', which is essentially forbidding others to reject us – a prohibition that is outside our control. The 'I *wish*' statement acknowledges that others have free will to make choices, even though their choices may hurt us.

CHALLENGING OUR THOUGHT PATTERNS

Another way to deal with our distorted or rigid thinking is to challenge it. If we find ourselves thinking, 'Other people should/ought to/must/have to …' we can ask ourselves, 'Why?' For example, if we think, 'Other people should show they love me, because if they don't, it means I'm of no value,' we can ask ourselves, 'Why *should* they?'

- *Scientifically*, is there evidence to say that others should love me? (No.)
- *Logically*, is there evidence that because I want this, it has to be so? (No.)
- *Pragmatically*, how will demanding that others 'should' do something help me reach my long-term healthy goal? (It won't.)

By challenging our thinking in this way, we repeat back to ourselves that there is no rational reason why everyone *should* like and appreciate us, whatever we do! Eventually, we will find our flawed/rigid thought patterns diminishing and being replaced by healthy ones, and by a recognition that it would be even more desirable that others like us for the person we are, rather than for what we do for them.

Diana, her two married daughters and all their children went on holiday together, sharing a spacious cottage. Diana insisted on cooking all the meals and doing everything for everyone. Nothing was too much trouble. Her internal voice was saying: 'I must do everything I can to give my family a good holiday, then I will feel that I'm being a good mum.' However, doing everything for everyone – in a strange place and an unfamiliar kitchen – made her so tired that one evening she lost her temper. This made her ask herself, 'What's the matter with me? I'm normally so tolerant of others.'

That evening, Diana was horrified to overhear her daughters talking about her: 'No wonder Mum's exhausted. She's always running around saying [mimicking], "No, you sit down – I'll do it."'

'Yes, she's her own worst enemy, always trying to please everyone. She's just not assertive enough!'

'And never saying what she really wants – she's impossible sometimes.'

'She means well!'

It seemed that all Diana's efforts to be a loving mother had backfired; she hadn't recognised the negative effect her 'help' was having on the family. Sometimes she had become aware that other people got annoyed with her for what seemed no reason at all, but she had just assumed that it was because she hadn't done enough to be helpful and supportive. When the truth finally hit her it sent her spiralling into depression. However, she underwent some counselling which helped her to uncover the roots of her need to people-please, and enabled her to change first her thinking and attitudes and then her behaviour, learning to be assertive. She realised that although her intentions were good, her methods were flawed. She also recognised the 'shoulds' on the internal tape running in her head: 'I should always be nice to everyone ...', 'I should be doing everything ...' and realised these 'rules' had come from her mother, who created a feeling of inadequacy in those she was trying to 'rescue' with her continual maternal 'niceness'. Diana finally realised that she was looking to others, rather than to God, for her sense of identity.

ACTIVITY
Look back to the examples of distorted thinking given at the beginning of the chapter.

- Note the thinking errors you recognise in yourself.
- Using those examples, what would be a more helpful thought? For example: All or nothing: 'I'll be seen as a bad person if I don't say I'll do it.' More helpful thought: 'Saying very occasionally that I can't do it doesn't make me a bad person. I still help out a lot of other times, and in God's sight I'm not bad; I'm His cherished child.'

REFLECTION
Consider your own thought patterns and see which of them are preventing you from growing into the person God wants you to be. Read 2 Corinthians 10:5 and reflect on ways in which you can 'take captive' your rigid and distorted thinking to 'to make it obedient to Christ'.

PRAYER
Lord Jesus, I acknowledge that some of my thinking is distorted and results in behaviour that doesn't glorify You. Please forgive me; help me to bring my thinking into line with Bible truth, and may that truth set me free to be the person You intend me to be. Amen.

CHAPTER 5

APPROVAL ADDICTION AND SELF-DEFEATING BEHAVIOUR

A bad habit is like a warm bed; easy to get into but hard to get out of.

(Irish proverb)

THE NEED FOR APPROVAL

Some Christians believe – and may even teach – that it's wrong or unhealthy to value the approval of others, but it is entirely normal to want to be liked by those whom we love and respect. God has made us, biologically and genetically, to look for approval from significant others. As we have seen, in childhood, approval from our parents and other authority figures is a reward for positive behaviour; this can continue into adult life, our behaviour as adults being shaped and influenced by the approval we received or did not receive as children. When we realise that the way we behave can give us the approval we thirst for, we can become people-pleasers, and as we gain approval by people-pleasing we redouble our efforts to please. This is understandable, but if our desire or need to seek approval from other people becomes more important to us than living in a way that brings God's approval, then it has become a problem, and we need to start working on a solution. We have already mentioned how we are, as God said to the prophet Jeremiah about the people of Israel, digging cisterns (or wells) in the wrong place (see Jer. 2:13).

Although behaving in non-assertive, people-pleasing ways can give us a 'fix' because we gain approval (affirmation, praise, acceptance, thanks, love) and avoid others' disapproval (criticism, rejection, put-downs, withholding of love), this powerful need for approval often causes people-pleasers to give up power and control in relationships with others. For Christian people-pleasers this frequently means that God is no longer on the throne of our lives: we have allowed someone else (the person we're trying to please) to usurp that place and become more powerful than God. As people-pleasers we choose to take on too much, spreading ourselves too thinly because we can't say no and find it difficult to delegate. Always saying yes to others' requests or demands, meeting others' needs and accepting blame are all habits which can become compulsive or addictive: as the proverb quoted at the start of this chapter says, a bad habit is easy to get into but hard to get out of. Approval addiction, like so many other addictions, results in health problems, low-self esteem and unhealthy relationships. It also has a spiritual hold over Christians because it gives Satan, the enemy, a foothold. In C.S. Lewis's *Screwtape Letters* an older, experienced devil gives advice to his younger nephew. In one letter, he remarks that he has noted that someone has become a Christian but that his old mental and physical habits still worked in the devils' favour. Habits are hard to break … and the enemy knows it!

A tendency to be 'nice' in order to avoid conflict and confrontation leaves us in the role of 'victim'. We need to realise that 'niceness' will not protect us from potential or actual abuse; we need to learn to *confront*. If, for one reason or another, we fear conflict and confrontation, we become conditioned to avoid any form of anger or conflict; this prevents us from addressing the roots of the fear, and from growing through the addressing.

PEOPLE-PLEASING PARTNERS

A major problem area for people-pleasers, addicted as we are to approval and ways of behaving to avoid disapproval, is that of intimate relationships. Female people-pleasers in particular can find themselves behaving in one of the following ways:

- Trying to manipulate a partners' approval by always pleasing him.
- Trying to meet his every need to prove he can't live without her: 'If I make him need me enough, he will never abandon me' (my deepest fear).
- Never confronting him or disagreeing with him.

All the above behaviours – and others – make for a one-sided and unhealthy relationship. The people-pleaser says, 'I love you because I need you' rather than 'I need you because I love you'. People-pleasing intimate relationships with men can chip away at women's identities.

We tend to assume that in an intimate relationship the non-assertive partner will be the woman and, although this is true in most cases, it's not always so. Take Jim, for example:

> Jim, a passive, unassuming man would 'go with the flow' for the sake of peace. His girlfriend of several years, who had been living with him at weekends, changed jobs to be nearer Jim's house and, without any discussion, moved in permanently with him. It just happened! Jim so wanted her approval and love that he accepted this arrangement without considering his own wellbeing. Several years and a baby later, his GP referred him for counselling because he was feeling stressed with irritable bowel syndrome (IBS). As Jim explored his distress and hidden frustration, he began to recognise the impact that his non-assertive behaviour had had not only on the relationship, but also on his health. The relationship went through a very rocky patch as Jim began to take note of his own desires and needs and to voice them assertively. A year later, Jim felt better about himself and was so much happier in the relationship that the couple decided to get married – and his IBS more or less disappeared.

A controlling or abusive man enjoys having a people-pleasing partner, whom he can mould at will. Like a cat with a mouse, the abusive/controlling man plays with the people-pleaser's identity, personhood and sense of self, wanting her to fit his 'fantasy'. If the woman permits this, she will gain nothing: the man will lose respect for her, may very well discard her, and she will finish up with her self-esteem badly eroded – or destroyed.

Sometimes where the man is a controller and the woman a people-pleaser, the sexual aspect of their relationship suffers because the man always calls the shots. You can imagine what may happen if the woman feels she always has to please her partner. The outcome is often a violation of her sexual and psychological boundaries. It's important for every woman to decide her own boundaries in these areas and consistently enforce them in a relationship. Some women routinely feign orgasm just to please their husbands, with the result that the husbands pat themselves on the back for their sexual prowess. If the woman doesn't have an orgasm, the controlling partner sees this as a failure on her part and blames her, belittling and even rejecting her. So a people-pleasing woman in that situation would try even harder to have an orgasm. Some non-assertive people with a history of sexual, physical or emotional abuse have been taught to be 'nice' and 'just keep quiet'. This leads directly to people-pleasing, especially in sexual matters.

REMEMBER
• God doesn't want us to change ourselves into the person our husband/boyfriend/partner wants us to be. He has made us uniquely who we are.
• If a man really loves us for who we are, he will not try and change us. He will want us to grow into our full potential.

People-pleasers often choose angry and aggressive partners because they have 'learnt to dance to the dance steps of their parents'. In other words, the model of adult relationships to which they have been exposed, although far from ideal, is a *known* one; they may not even realise that there are alternative, healthier and more positive ways of relating to another adult in an intimate relationship. Therefore, if the female people-pleaser has had an angry father and an appeasing mother, she might grow up to choose to marry an aggressive man and become the appeaser herself. If she has been brought up in a home where there is much anger, she might have used passivity as a means of survival. She may then choose a passive role in a marriage relationship, and become the wife of a controlling, angry, dominating man.

In these situations, the chosen angry or aggressive partners can project their own sense of inferiority onto the people-pleaser. However, remember Eleanor Roosevelt's famous (and accurate) remark that no one can make you feel inferior without your permission!

PEOPLE-PLEASING THOSE IN AUTHORITY

Some of us who are addicted to acceptance and approval and find it hard to be assertive may find ourselves in work situations where we are bullied and abused.

> Jo worked with a very critical, demanding boss. She felt too frightened to tell him that she thought he was making unreasonable demands on her to meet unrealistic deadlines. All her relationships were based on gaining approval, and this was the first time in her life she had encountered a relationship where approval couldn't be earned. Jo became more and more anxious and was eventually signed off work. Learning assertiveness skills and to manage her anxiety helped Jo to feel less afraid of her boss.

HOW TO CHANGE

We can't change our partners/bosses, but we *can* change ourselves. By refusing to accept or allow negative behaviour – put-downs, criticism and anger – we are changing, slowly but surely, from being people-pleasers into people who are assertive. If we go on being 'nice' in such circumstances, we are rewarding our partners/bosses for abusing us, and they will go on doing so. To paraphrase Dennis Wholey,[1] expecting a partner to treat us fairly because we are nice people is like expecting the bull not to charge because we are vegetarians! We need to start by changing just one thought, feeling or response … inch by inch, not yard by yard. If this applies to you:

- Don't 'give permission' to your partner/boss to treat you badly.
- Don't believe that what someone says to you to make you feel inferior is the truth.
- Remind yourself of God's truth – '… you are precious and honoured in my sight, and … I love you' (Isa. 43:4) – and listen to that, not to negatives from the person trying to belittle you.
- Don't be willing to take the blame for something that isn't your responsibility by always saying 'I'm sorry' in generalised terms.
- Don't allow the other person always to be right – that means you are always wrong! This will badly affect your self-esteem.

NOTE: If your intimate personal relationship is distressing, we would urge you to seek help – see the list of helpful websites and organisations at the end of this book.[2]

ACTIVITY

HOW MUCH DO YOU NEED APPROVAL?
By now, you will hopefully know the 'right' response to the statements below! Try to be honest with yourself!

- If others don't approve of me, I feel worthless.
- I need everyone to like me.

- I need the approval of others to feel loved and happy.
- My self-esteem depends upon others liking me.
- Thinking others disapprove of me can keep me awake at night.
- I look to others for approval before I make important decisions.
- I feel worthless when others criticise me.
- To be liked is essential to my wellbeing.

REFLECTION

Non-assertive, people-pleasing behaviour is learned behaviour – but what has been learned can be unlearned. We have seen that people-pleasing is learned from role models (a parent who was a people-pleaser, for example), through the rewards it brings ('If I make puddings for the church lunch, people will approve of me'), and through negative reinforcement ('I avoid the unpleasantness of conflict, anger and confrontation if I do what people want'). So, to *unlearn* the need for approval we can try to *accept* the following:

- I am of great value to God.
- God loves me, unconditionally, just as I am.
- I don't have to prove anything to God to make Him love me.
- I can't gain approval all the time.
- Trying to please others constantly won't make me feel good about myself long-term.
- I don't like everyone, so I needn't worry if someone doesn't like me.
- Some people may not approve of me because of their own issues, not mine – it's not necessarily my fault!
- I can choose to change my behaviour.

PRAYER

Father God, my pain and fear of not being accepted and approved by others frightens me. Please let Your love flow deeper than my fear and pain. Release within me the gift of boldness, and the courage to leave behind my people-pleasing tendencies, so becoming more assertive. Thank You, Lord. Amen.

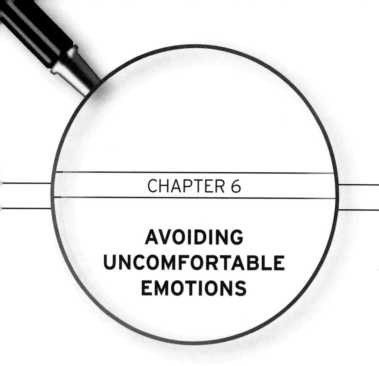

CHAPTER 6

AVOIDING UNCOMFORTABLE EMOTIONS

Anger is the emotional reaction that signals something is wrong and that you might get hurt.

(Harriet B. Braiker)[1]

We have already said that we often become people-pleasers to protect ourselves from uncomfortable emotions. David Burns, a cognitive therapist, uses the word 'emotophobia' to express an irrational or excessive fear of uncomfortable or negative feelings. Emotophobia prevents us from saying no when that is what we really want to say. In this chapter, we will look at our fears of our own and other people's anger and other disturbing emotions from which we try to protect ourselves.

A fear of anger can develop for several different reasons: for many people it's buried in childhood trauma; for instance, an occasion when a significant carer displayed aggression or explosive anger. To young children this is terrifying: children need adults to model effective behaviour, including that of being in control, so if a significant adult displays 'out of control' behaviour such as aggressive anger, children's trust is undermined and they rapidly learn that anger is to be avoided at all costs. If, to keep the peace, a mother responds passively to a husband's violence, children see anger expressed as passivity in the mother and as aggression in the abusive father. So they never learn from adults to express or manage anger appropriately, and adopt 'survival strategies' to cope – but these are not constructive strategies; instead, they lead to the people-pleasing tendencies we have already considered: trying to please others to avoid conflict.

Anger has a lot of negative connotations for many people, several arising, as we have seen, from our childhood experiences. Sometimes we have been brought up with the idea that all anger is 'bad', though when we look at the Gospels we see that Jesus was angry on several occasions – for example, when He overturned the cheating money-changers' tables in the Temple. In considering the fact that many people-pleasers fear anger, we perhaps need to distinguish between a fear of *our own* anger, and the fear of *someone else's* anger. The two are connected, of course, but different. Whose anger do you fear? A parent's? (Are you still hearing an angry parent's voice when you don't come up to your own, or to their, standards?) An authority figure's? (Has a teacher, a church leader, a boss or someone else in a position of responsibility been angry with you and made you feel worthless or foolish or humiliated?) Your own? (You're not sure if it's OK to be angry, so you try not to acknowledge it; or you realise you're angry, but don't know what to do with that anger because no one has ever modelled to you how to express it appropriately.)

PEOPLE-PLEASERS FEAR THEIR OWN ANGER

Many people-pleasers fear their own anger because their thinking about anger is flawed. We have perhaps been brought up to believe that all anger is wrong, so if we feel angry we assume that we are bad people and try to push the anger down and ignore it. Or we may be afraid to express anger in case we are rejected, or because we feel it's not 'nice' to be angry. How do we deal with this?

For a start, it's important to recognise that anger is not always bad. Jesus was rightly angry at the way the cheating money-changers were acting in the Temple but, quite apart from the example of Jesus, when we look at history we can see that many great reforms were the result of the right kind of anger. For instance, William Wilberforce was so angry about the horrors and abuses of the eighteenth- and nineteenth-century British slave trade that he channelled his anger into getting it abolished. Anger, even on a much smaller scale, can be healthy and we need to give ourselves permission to feel it. Feeling angry is neither right nor wrong, good nor bad, negative nor positive – it just is. Anger is often viewed, however, as black or white, on or off, all or nothing. People are perceived as either calm and in control or angry, upset, agitated and, therefore, out of control.

In her book *The Disease to Please*, Harriet B. Braiker says, 'Anger is the emotional reaction that signals something is wrong and that you might get hurt.'[2] As human beings we are not morally accountable for having emotions – including anger – because this is how God has created us. It's important to accept that anger is normal for everyone. Resisting any form of anger, perhaps by focusing on guilt ('I'm so bad because I feel angry!') is not helpful and may lead to our subsequently feeling depressed ('I'm a horrible person to feel angry like this'). Neither is it helpful to repress our anger – to pretend it's not there, and push it under the surface. Whilst feeling angry is not wrong in itself, the crucial issue is how we handle that anger, ie what we do with it. If I get angry and hit someone, then that aggressive expression of my anger would be wrong, but the anger provoking the act wouldn't necessarily be so. *Our moral accountability over anger is in relation to the way we choose to express it.* As people-pleasers we need to learn to *acknowledge* our anger (in other words, we shouldn't pretend that we're not angry when, for example, someone takes advantage of us or criticises us unfairly), to *accept* it (it's OK to feel angry sometimes) and to *express* it appropriately.

CASE STUDY 1

What can happen if anger is expressed inappropriately – ie projected onto other people.

Sam's boss is annoyed. His wife has forgotten to pick up his dry-cleaning. So after work he has a go at Sam about a delayed project for which Sam is responsible. Sam doesn't answer back (because people are being made redundant in the firm), even though he's seething inside because he knows, and his boss knows, that the delays are out of Sam's control. Sam's anger bubbles away beneath the surface on his way home and he's still feeling irritable on arriving at his house. His wife, Alison, innocently remarks, 'You're late, dear!' and Sam explodes. She's angry that he shouted at her for no reason and bangs about in the kitchen getting the evening meal. One of the children comes in to report a conflict over TV channels. Alison marches into the living room, switches off the television and shouts at the children to go upstairs and tidy their rooms instead of wasting time on rubbish TV. The eldest, furious at being denied his favourite sports programme, kicks his little brother on his sullen way upstairs; the little brother, unable to take out his frustration on anyone else, then slyly kicks the dog …

Obviously the above is a good example of how *not* to handle anger! It demonstrates that inappropriate expressions of anger can lead to a chain of bad feeling and frustration. What can we do instead? Occasionally we don't need (or it's impossible) to say anything to the person with whom we feel angry. However, anger towards someone else, especially if that person is a close relation, often (though not always) needs to be expressed. Sometimes people hide their anger in the belief that by doing so they can protect the relationship. In fact the reverse is true. If you hide your anger, the other person has no way of knowing that you are angry, and so can't choose to act differently in future.

Sometimes our anger may be directed at ourselves – for example, for saying yes when we would rather have said no. In these situations we can sometimes express anger appropriately by writing it down, by walking it off, by punching a cushion … or by taking it to the foot of the cross and leaving it with Jesus. We are thus acknowledging and expressing our anger, which is healthier than ignoring or suppressing it.

CASE STUDY 2
Below is a scenario with two possible outcomes – a) and b). Here we can see ways of dealing with our own anger.

It's Friday morning before school; I'm running slightly late, have PMT and feel tired and irritable. As I try simultaneously to get two pairs of children's shoes onto the correct feet, wipe the baby's face and hands before she smears porridge everywhere, and find a lost reading book, the phone rings. It's a friend, asking me – for the third time in two weeks – if I could possibly take her children to school with mine as she's not feeling well (I suspect she's pregnant but hasn't told me yet). I am absolutely furious because I feel she's taken advantage of me – again.

a) *I say yes* – because I never say no. I then feel under even more pressure because now, as well as getting my own three children organised, I also have to go up the road (in the opposite direction from school) with them and then return with five in tow – again! I feel angry and put upon, and guilty for feeling as I do. I also feel even more pressured because time is tight, so I snap at my own children, which will also make me feel guilty later (when I have time to reflect) because it's not their fault. On reaching my friend's house, however, I'm all sweetness and light, hiding my anger and reinforcing the impression she already has of me as a 'soft touch'. I'm not too stressed to notice that she doesn't look anything like as unwell as I feel. I take her children to school with mine, yet again.

Result: When I get home I feel stressed, angry, resentful, hypocritical, put upon and guilty – not a good start to the morning! And because I haven't expressed my anger appropriately, it may well still be there, under the surface, waiting to explode at an inappropriate moment.

b) *I say no* – because I've read a bit of this book and decide to try putting it into practice. I tell my friend, 'I'm glad you felt you could ask me, but I really can't do it this morning. I'm feeling lousy and running behind schedule myself. Maybe you should just wait till you feel a bit better and take the children to school late for once.'

Result: I have taken a step in the right direction: I've said no; I haven't apologised, but I've explained that I'm not feeling well myself, ie I have my own needs to consider. I may have to deal with a feeling of (inappropriate and unnecessary) guilt later, but I won't have to deal with pent-up anger towards my friend; in addition, my children won't be on the receiving end of my stress and frustration. (I could also make a mental note never to answer the phone in the ten minutes before I have to leave to take the children to school.)

HOW TO HANDLE OUR OWN ANGER

- Recognise early physical signs of anger – faster heartbeat, tense muscles, laboured breathing, bloating, migraine and psychological clues – irritability, feeling stressed, mood swings.
- Use anger-management strategies such as controlled breathing and relaxation (See *Insight into Anger*).[3]
- Express anger constructively and clearly – the goal is to convey accurate information.
- Assume responsibility for your own anger, ie use 'I' not 'you' – see below.
- Do not use threatening gestures.
- Speak slowly and calmly.

It is better to say: 'I feel angry when you do that, because I sense you don't value my opinions' because this is an appropriate and non-aggressive way of conveying your anger; whereas saying: 'You make me so angry. How dare you take advantage of me again?' is likely to put the other person's back up.

Being unable to say no can cause us to become strangers to our own anger so that we fear allowing it to surface in case we lose control. Learning to handle our own anger is therefore very valuable. Denying and suppressing our anger gives rise to physical and psychological ill-health, because ignoring or burying anger doesn't make it go away. It will always be there, 'buried alive', so that over time our inner world can become like a volcano waiting to erupt with rage and hysteria. Repressed anger, ie anger which is denied and suppressed, can also result in our being trapped in unsatisfactory relationships by a self-imposed vicious circle of not wanting to hurt other people's feelings.

PEOPLE-PLEASERS FEAR OTHER PEOPLE'S ANGER

It's important to realise that people-pleasing can become habitual, not only because we try to protect ourselves from our own uncomfortable emotions, but also because we may be so frightened of another person's anger that we avoid any kind of conflict. In both cases we can't say no!

When Sarah was a child, she lived in a home with a violent and alcoholic father and a very critical mother who abused Sarah verbally when Sarah did anything to displease her. When Sarah's father was angry he would become violently abusive with her, hitting her hard for not doing what he said. As a result, Sarah learned to avoid angry responses from her parents by not doing anything that would provoke their anger. Her parent-pleasing behaviour as a child and adolescent in that situation protected her from harm to herself. However, it became a habitual part of Sarah's life, carrying on into adulthood. When older, Sarah used this same people-pleasing strategy in order to protect herself from the anger of an aggressive and verbally abusive husband (like so many victims of abuse, she may have unconsciously chosen to marry someone abusive). By means of this people-pleasing strategy, Sarah avoided all marital conflict which might potentially harm her and damage the marriage. Obviously this was not a healthy, happy relationship, and Sarah ended up as a passive, conflict-avoiding 'doormat'.

(Perhaps ironically, the 'Sarah model' of relating to another person or other people can sometimes be perceived by others as manipulative and controlling because one's persistent 'niceness' and 'conflict-avoiding' behaviour is seen as a passive-aggressive way of keeping one's distance, instead of enjoying an intimate relationship in which emotions are aired. So, whilst people-pleasing behaviour to avoid an angry response may reduce anxiety and fears in the short term, in the long term, fears of intense, uncomfortable emotions will only intensify.)

Because people-pleasers almost always fear and avoid uncomfortable emotions not only within themselves but, in particular, those of other people, especially anger, this can set up a pattern of behaviour which is described overleaf:

As people-pleasers we fear another person's anger

So ...

We avoid conflict and confrontation

So ...

We keep saying yes (even though often we'd rather say no)

So ...

We feel angry but don't express that anger

So ...

It gets bottled up inside us as resentment and bitterness

So ...

We feel stressed and eventually may suffer migraines, high blood
pressure etc ...

Or explode!

As mentioned previously it's important to realise that people-pleasing can become habitual not only because we try to protect ourselves from our own uncomfortable emotions (ie we deny that we're angry, or we're too 'nice' to say 'I feel angry' for fear of what others may think of us), but also because we may be so frightened of another person's anger that we avoid any kind of conflict; in both cases we can't say no.

Look at the vicious circle opposite: the people-pleasers find themselves in a relationship which is unsatisfactory for some reason, but can't end it because they fear the anger of the other person in the relationship.

Relationship

Unhappy, dissatisfied

Want to end relationship

Fear ending relationship will make other person angry

Fear the dreaded confrontation – lack courage so continue people-pleasing

OTHER UNCOMFORTABLE EMOTIONS

Lack of assertiveness almost always stems from lack of self-esteem. As people-pleasers, we can feel so 'unworthy' and 'flawed' that we *expect* to be rejected by others. Several factors can give rise to these feelings of unworthiness; there may be a physical reason such as being perceived as spotty or overweight, or having a deformity or disability of some kind. (Chris O was profoundly deafened some years ago and that totally sapped her confidence when interacting with people she doesn't know.) There may be a psychological flaw – we may feel we are stupid, or uneducated, or poor or we may feel ashamed or embarrassed about our family background. Any of these reasons – and others like them – can lead to feelings of inferiority or worthlessness and an expectation of being rejected by other people.

This can become a self-fulfilling prophecy: we start by *thinking* we may be rejected; then we begin *expecting* to be rejected and then we *project onto others* our own negative feelings about ourselves – and can then actually *be* rejected because of the vibes we are giving off!

People who feel 'unworthy' are afraid of rejection and similar uncomfortable emotions such as being disliked, (false) guilt at being perceived as selfish, (false) guilt about upsetting others, as well as anger, which we have already discussed. They feel inadequate to handle conflict and confrontation and/or overwhelmed by hostility and aggression, so they continue in their people-pleasing habits as a protection against these emotions. What's the answer? Learning to handle uncomfortable emotions and to manage conflict and confrontation constructively can help us overcome our tendency to be people-pleasers. This may not be as straightforward as it sounds, because it takes courage to face our fears, especially when our very identity may have been built on avoiding them. The emotions we fear can seem like monsters – terrifying and larger than life – because they are invariably hidden behind the façade of people-pleasing.

So, although we may not be aware of it, we often say yes to requests and demands (when we'd really rather say no) in order to protect ourselves against one or more of the uncomfortable emotions already mentioned. We are afraid that if we say no we may find ourselves struggling with *guilt* about letting people down, or we may fear the *anger* and conflict that could arise should someone challenge our refusal; we may fear facing up to a deep sense of *worthlessness*, because saying yes boosts our self-esteem, whereas saying no takes it down several notches. All these are symptoms of the condition described in the first paragraph of the chapter – we are emotophobic.

Every time we say yes when we'd rather say no, we give way to our fears of uncomfortable emotions to protect ourselves from anxiety, but the short-term reduction in anxiety actually only increases our long-term people-pleasing tendencies. The fear of hurting someone else's feelings or provoking their anger or disapproval drives us to be people-pleasers. We 'predict' (or jump to the conclusion) that others will become angry or reject us if we say no, or we 'mind read' and assume that others will be hurt – so we say yes, even though deep down we don't want to, simply to defend ourselves against disturbing emotions that we've never learned to handle or manage.

Another unwelcome consequence of 'being nice' (or people-pleasing) is that we may not recognise that we are being exploited as people take advantage of our desire to please. Even when we do recognise this we may say nothing because of a deep-seated desire to avoid conflict at all costs. For at the core of our 'niceness' is a fear of uncomfortable emotions and situations; yet uncomfortable feelings are part of our human DNA. We are biologically programmed to feel hurt, anger and fear and to respond defensively when we believe others are about to hurt us or those we love.

We may, consciously or unconsciously, believe that by 'being nice' we can keep everything on an even keel and avoid uncomfortable situations and emotions. So we use our 'niceness' as a kind of psychological armour to protect ourselves from what we think of as 'destructive' emotions in ourselves and others. Subconsciously we're saying to ourselves, 'If I'm nice, no one will be angry with me or reject me.' By concentrating on 'being nice' we don't allow ourselves even to feel, let alone express, any uncomfortable emotions towards others, but in doing this we are not being transparent or real.

Fear and avoidance of uncomfortable feelings pull us into people-pleasing habits and the inability to be assertive – to say no. If you are not an assertive person, you will no doubt have become adept at buffering yourself against confrontation and conflict, but in order to overcome fears of any kind we have to be exposed to them. Think of a person who has always been afraid to learn to drive. (Chris L once worked with someone like this.) Over time the fear of learning to drive develops into a fear of going on the roads, so fear of accidents increases and becomes more likely to be self-fulfilling. The only way to overcome that fear is to confront it face on and learn to drive a car – in small, achievable steps. So, to overcome our fear (or even phobia) of uncomfortable emotions, we need to give ourselves the opportunity to learn to handle conflict and confrontation and their accompanying emotions, instead of always pleasing others to keep the peace and avoid those emotions.

So, as we can see, the emotophobic's protection strategy against uncomfortable feelings and situations is to say yes all the time. This seems to work, because we avoid feeling guilty, but of course there is a price to pay – and a vicious circle! It works like this: We can be overwhelmed with (unexpressed) resentment and anger towards the person who so effectively manipulated our 'niceness' that once again we said yes; then we feel guilty and ashamed of harbouring those feelings of resentment; we then try to avoid the friends who see us as easy targets for getting us to do anything they want; but then we feel unloved because we have no contact with our friends; so we seek them out once more, and the cycle repeats itself:

Request

Can't say no –
so grant request

Feel resentful, and
ashamed of this feeling

Become angry with self

Self-critical voice:
'I must be mad! I never wanted
to do it in the first place.'

Avoid friends

Feel lonely and unworthy
without friends so
seek them out again

Another vicious circle in which people-pleasers can find themselves trapped through their fear of anger, conflict or confrontation is shown below: it's the 'peace at any price' circle. This is frequently found in an employment situation.

Abused, harassed, exploited

Keep quiet and stay in job

Want to complain or resign

Fear of confrontation; fear that if we're honest, the boss will be angry and may even discipline us

Lack courage to be honest

Don't want to annoy/hurt boss (ie peace at any price)

LEARNING TO SAY NO

So, to conclude: in the short term, people-pleasing promotes a feel-good factor, but the long-term payoff is ill-health and burnout. The answer to the people-pleasing syndrome is learning to say no! Saying no requires us to start looking to God, rather than to other people, for our sense of self-worth.

ACTIVITY

Look at the following to determine to what extent you are 'emotophobic'. How many can you put your hand up to?

- I become very upset when it appears that others are angry with me.
- I always try to avoid confrontation.
- When I am hurt and angry I tend to go off in a quiet and sullen mood.
- I feel responsible for controlling how other people feel.
- I think showing love means never getting angry or being in conflict with others.
- When others are aggressive around me I am likely to experience physical problems such as headaches, skin rashes, stomach pains etc.
- Difficulties are better left undiscussed – they'll sort themselves out in time.
- I always smile and cover up my true feelings – who cares whether or not I'm angry?
- I believe that if someone gets angry with me it must be my fault.
- I would never disagree with or challenge someone else's opinion because I'm afraid I may trigger a conflict. (And, of course, I can't handle conflicts.)
- In a restaurant I'd never send back an unsatisfactory meal.
- I dislike returning goods to a shop in case they don't believe me.
- I get anxious about complaining if I've been overcharged.

REFLECTION

Think of a time when you engaged in people-pleasing, either in a relationship or in a work situation, because you feared exposure to uncomfortable emotions. Ask God to help you:

- Explore your thoughts and motives.
- Explore your intentions and actions.
- Did you fail to communicate your feelings? Can you see why?
- What would you like to do differently if you found yourself in that situation again?

PRAYER

Lord, thank You that You love me just as I am right now. Thank You for showing me that I am vulnerable in some of these areas. Please help me to learn to recognise my own anger and express it appropriately, to confront my fears of uncomfortable emotions, to manage conflict and to grow into the person You long for me to be. Amen.

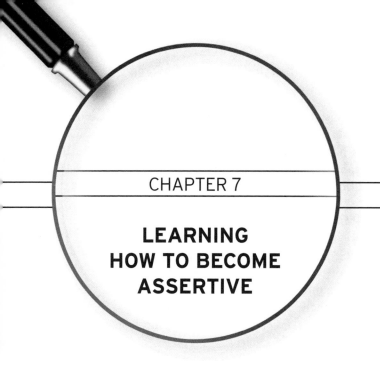

CHAPTER 7

LEARNING
HOW TO BECOME
ASSERTIVE

The most useful piece of learning for the uses of life is to unlearn what is untrue.

(Antisthenes)

Because non-assertive people find it hard to say no, turning instead into people-pleasers (saying yes most of the time), we need to *unlearn* some of the things that make us habitually say yes – the tyranny of 'should' and 'must', for example – and to replace them with *learned* assertiveness skills. In this chapter, we're going to suggest several different assertiveness strategies that you might find helpful to adopt.

HOW TO SAY NO
When you are given an invitation, or asked to do something, or

someone demands something of you, as a non-assertive people-pleaser you will almost automatically say yes, because saying yes has become a habit or a conditioned reflex. It's therefore important to learn to *break the habit of saying yes immediately* – especially when you know you'd rather say no!

TIME OUT

Give yourself time to make a considered response. This will enable you to delay your answer in order to:

- Think through your choices.
- Explore the likely outcome of each choice.
- Choose the option that sits most comfortably with your truest self – the 'godly' choice.
- Respond as appropriate – yes/no/counter-proposal or compromise.

HANDLING TIME OUT

Try to break the conversation in order to take time out. If face to face, at work for example:

- Try to remove yourself physically for a few minutes to break the automatic 'yes' response.
  - Make an excuse to go to the bathroom.
  - Go and get a drink.
  - Leave the office.

- Tell the person making the request that you need some time to think about what they've asked before you can give them an answer. You might say:

- 'Thanks for the invitation. I haven't got my diary with me. I'll check later today and get back to you with an answer.'
- 'I'm not sure if I'll have time to do that; I'll have to see if I can change things and get back to you tomorrow/next week.'
- 'Let me come back to you with an answer when I've looked at my work schedule.'
- 'I'd really like to do this with you, but I'm not sure if I'm free on that day. I'll tell you tomorrow.'
- 'I'm not sure how this will fit in with the family's activities, so I'll get back to you this evening.'

If you are on the phone:

- May I call you back in a few minutes?
- Can I ask you to hold for a moment whilst I just check my diary?

In order to get these 'time out phrases' into your head and onto your tongue, write them out in a way that comes naturally to you (ie in the kind of phrase you would normally use), together with any others you can think of, and practise them by saying them out loud.

Sometimes people demand an immediate response (especially if you've always said yes straightaway before).

'STUCK RECORD' TECHNIQUE
Here's a short vignette demonstrating what is known as the 'stuck record' technique, which may help you when you find yourself in a similar situation:

Workmate (on telephone): Hi Carol, I need to ask you a big favour. Can you do my shift next Saturday? A friend's invited me to watch the football.

Carol: Can you hang on a minute?

Workmate: Yes – sure!

Carol (reminds herself of the 'time out phrases' on a card in her pocket): Hello again. I think I may have something already in my diary, so I'll get back to you tomorrow, when I know what Frank's doing.

Workmate: I can't wait until tomorrow – we have to tell the boss today. You always ...

Carol: I know it's frustrating that I can't give you an answer immediately, but l need to check with Frank first.

Workmate: Can't you get hold of him now? You always change shifts for me.

Carol: I realise how much you want to go to the match and I'd like to help you out, but Frank's in a meeting all day and I can't check with his diary until late this evening, so I'll let you know tomorrow.

Important principles of using 'stuck record' technique:

• Empathise with the other person
• Paraphrase their feelings and repeat back to them.

Don't worry if this feels awkward at first – skills have to be learnt!

THINK THROUGH YOUR CHOICES

Non-assertive people become accustomed to assuming that when someone asks them to do something the only possible answer is yes. But there are two other possibilities: the first is no – when that really is the best choice – and the second is a compromise: modify the request/demand so that your own interests and needs are also met. For example, if the church office asks you to help in the book shop for five hours, you could respond by saying you can only offer two. However, beware of using a compromise to avoid saying no, when you really haven't got time to help in the book shop at all, or don't want to, or don't feel it's the best use of your time! In other words, don't use a compromise to avoid saying no, simply in order to protect yourself from rejection, anger or disapproval.

EXPLORE THE LIKELY OUTCOME OF EACH CHOICE

Take a blank piece of paper and divide it into three columns with headings:

If I say yes   *If I say no*   *If I say … (alternative choice)*

Next, in each column list reasons in favour (gains) and reasons against (costs). Then evaluate the costs and gains against how the final decision will affect *you*, not how it will affect the person making the request.

Learning to be assertive means leaving behind some people-pleasing habits, but it doesn't mean that instead of automatically saying yes, you will now always automatically say no! It's about making the best choice for your health, and thinking through your options carefully and in a considered way during your 'time out'.

CHOOSE YOUR FAVOURED OPTION

- Make a conscious choice in the light of your own needs.
- Decide on an option because you *want* to do it, rather than because you feel you *ought* to.
- Stick to your decision graciously but firmly, even if the person making the request tries to persuade you to think again.

If your chosen option is to say no:
If, after weighing up the pros and cons in the light of your own needs, you decide that you will say no to the request:

- Respond firmly and honestly, eg, 'I'm calling back about doing your shift for you on Saturday. I won't be able to do it for you this time, because it turns out that something else is already in our diary.'

If this seems a little too 'brusque' or 'not you', you could use what has been called 'the sandwich technique'. This is where you 'sandwich' your no between two affirming, or complimentary, or positive statements.

- I value our friendship (*positive*) and I know this will upset you, but I'm calling back to say I won't be able to do your shift on Saturday (*negative*). If I could, I would (*positive*). I hope you understand.
- I appreciate your asking me to do that with you (*positive*), but this time I won't be able to come (*negative*). I hope you'll think of me again (*positive*).

Avoid:
- Apologising for saying 'no'.
- Getting into a debate about your decision.
- Thinking you have to justify or explain or excuse your 'no'.
- Expecting the other person to be angry with you, because then you may become defensive.

Finally, congratulate yourself that you have been able to say no!

If your chosen option is to offer a compromise:
If, after weighing all the options, you decide that you can *partly* comply with the request that has been made, you could offer your compromise using what is known as 'the "back to front" sandwich technique'. With this technique, you sandwich your chosen option between two negative messages.

- I'm calling back about doing your shift on Saturday, to let you know that I can't do it all day (*negative*). But if the boss agrees, I could come in to do the afternoon for you (*offering compromise – positive*). If that won't work, then I'm afraid I just can't do it at all (*negative*).

If the response from the person who's made the request is something like this: 'Oh no! It's a 1pm kick-off, and I won't be able to get there if you can only do the afternoon. I was counting on you to help me, Carol' (*emotional blackmail*), you need to stick to your guns.

- Don't negotiate ('Well, perhaps I could come in at midday if the boss agrees.')

- Don't threaten.
- Be friendly, but don't be persuaded/bullied into changing your mind.
- Be assertive but not aggressive, eg, 'You know I'm normally happy to change shifts, but this coming Saturday I can only manage the afternoon. If that's no good, then I'm afraid I can't help.'

CONFLICT MANAGEMENT

All relationships – good and bad – involve a measure of conflict. The key issue is how that conflict is managed. In poor relationships, conflict is viewed (and conducted) as a power struggle or control issue with a winner/loser mentality: so either I win and you lose, or you win and I lose. Adopting such a winner-takes-all stance is destructive to the relationship, because any conflict tends to deteriorate first into a power struggle and then into a battle of words accompanied by personal accusations and even threats. By contrast, in a good relationship, conflicts are handled constructively for the sake of the relationship, and resolved by finding mutual understanding and choosing to benefit the interests of the relationship. In other words, handling conflict constructively means the parties involved work together for the advancement of the relationship.

DESTRUCTIVE CONFLICT MANAGEMENT

- Uses accusatory, exaggerated words: 'You always/never …'
- One participant withdraws from the discussion, refusing to engage in verbal input.
- The other person is perceived as a competitor/rival/enemy and the only goal is to win the point/argument.
- Disagreements are characterised by stubborn and rigid adherence to the speaker's point of view, and an unwillingness to look at it from any other angle.
- There is an atmosphere of mutual distrust.
- Each blames the other and doesn't take responsibility for own actions: 'You make me feel so silly/angry/stupid.'
- The mood is hostile and anger is expressed aggressively.
- Brings up historical problems: 'You're just like your mother/father.'
- Uses threats such as: 'I am going to separate from/divorce you.'
- Uses the 'If … you would … ' formula: 'If you really loved me, you would …' 'If you cared about your work, you would …'
- Inflicts upset and hurt on other/s involved, engendering low self-esteem.
- Usually ends without resolution or moving forward – participants remain stuck in patterns of incitement and accusation.

Conflict usually begins at Level 1 and is normally *over or about behaviour,* ie about what someone has done or said, or about what they habitually do and say, until a breaking point is reached and a conflict is triggered. The conflict may then proceed to Level 2, which is *over and about the principles, values, rules and beliefs* that characterise a relationship. Such principles give rise to expectations of how individuals should be treated in a relationship.

People-pleasers not only protect themselves from rejection and anger, but also from misunderstandings and disapproval. Because emotions can be so highly charged in a conflict situation, others may not hear us and thus misinterpret what we are saying.

ADVICE FOR CONSTRUCTIVE CONFLICT MANAGEMENT

- Don't attack the other person with emotional abuse.
- Don't allow the collapse of the bond that holds the relationship together.
- Give time to talking out differences of expectations, values, thoughts, feelings etc.
- Maintain a friendly approach in discussion and be flexible enough to look at the issue from the other person's perspective.
- Reaffirm commitment to, and positive feelings about, the relationship.
- Affirm mutual trust.
- Don't use blame as a weapon.
- Separate the facts from the feelings associated with personal attack.
- Take responsibility for your own feelings: 'When you shout at me, I feel hurt.'
- Use the A, B, C and D communication approach: A = Explaining what the problem is; B = How I feel; C = What I'd like to suggest; D = How that will help the situation. For example 'When you throw things around and shout at me (A), I feel frightened (B). Please say what you want to say more calmly (C); then I would

feel less frightened and be able to think rationally again (D).'
- Attempt to remain neutral and objective.
- Listen carefully and clarify the other person's statements by reflecting back what you are hearing: 'If I understand you correctly, you're saying you feel …'; 'So, what you're saying is …'
- Don't make a value judgment about the validity of the other person's feelings, so *don't* say things like: 'You shouldn't be feeling like this – it's utter nonsense'; 'You're overreacting again!'
- Find the compromise that best serves the wishes of those involved.
- Keep the boundaries of conflict resolution to the confines of the issue in question, so if the conversation is getting onto dangerous ground and pulling in other issues, say something like, 'I think we're getting off track. Let's go back. Tell me again how you perceive this problem …'; 'Let's stop and see where we've got to; I know we both want to reach an acceptable solution.'
- Ask for suggestions about how to communicate in a way that doesn't hurt the other person: 'So, when I honestly tell you I don't like what you are wearing, you say your feelings are hurt. What would you like me to say instead?'
- Aim for a safe and productive discussion with a resolution based on deeper mutual understanding.
- Always, and throughout, affirm love and respect.

TIME OUT AS A TECHNIQUE FOR CONFLICT MANAGEMENT

This is an effective means to help yourself calm down, and it can prevent a minor conflict escalating into a full-blown argument. Time out provides an opportunity to interrupt and control a conflict. It isn't about 'giving in' or 'running away'.

Identify the early signs that your, or someone else's, emotions are starting to spiral out of control, such as a high-pitched voice, louder or faster speech, use of hostile language or accusatory gestures (pointing finger, clenched fist etc).

Ask for a period of time out, using prepared and rehearsed 'exit lines', for example:

- 'I need time to think about this. Can we resume the conversation in a quarter of an hour/this evening/tomorrow on the phone?'
- 'I'm beginning to feel really angry and I don't want to lose my temper and say things I might regret. So I'm going to take some time out for … /to calm down. Then, when I come back, we can have a constructive conversation and resolve this.'
- 'This discussion's becoming heated and I can't listen properly when I'm angry, so I'm going to go for a walk for five minutes to calm down.'

If possible, before the discussion starts get the other person/s involved to agree to the time out technique. If you don't, others may be furious that you are trying to stop a heated argument: 'Nobody walks out on me when I have something to say!' Don't rise to the bait or get defensive; try to defuse the anger.

- 'I understand that you feel angry because I'm walking away. I respect myself and you too much to say things I may regret. I'm giving myself some time to calm down, so that when I come back we can work this out like two reasonable, mature adults.'
- 'I understand you're feeling surprised, but I don't have to stay and listen to you shouting at me, so, when I come back,

hopefully we can talk about this rationally.'

Leave (without making a dramatic exit – provocative gestures, slamming doors etc). Don't fight to get out of the room. If the way is blocked, take time out by 'leaving' the conversation instead, and refusing to speak until you feel calmer.

- 'There's no point in trying to keep me here. I need time out to cool down.'
- 'I promise I'll come back and we'll resume the conversation.'

Use your time out constructively. Don't brood, rehearse anger responses, throw things or phone a friend to have them validate your position. Anger is highly contagious so use the time to calm down by means of relaxation and breathing exercises. (Physiologically, it takes twenty minutes for our bodies to calm down before we can be rational again after becoming angry.)

This is very important – a must. *Return to the situation with a genuine desire to resolve the conflict.* Ask others involved if they are also ready to resume. If things go off track again, take more time out.

MAKING EXITS

When you have had enough of an interaction (if someone is 'going on' at you, for instance), you need to be assertive and use some tactical goal-setting. Make a deadline for yourself or for the person 'going on at you' by setting a time limit: 'I only have five minutes to spare.' During that time, gradually withdraw eye contact and, when the five minutes are up, interrupt the flow of words non-verbally (eg by putting a hand on the speaker's shoulder) and verbally, making eye contact and saying something like, 'Excuse me. I really have to go now.' If the speaker tries to extend the time, move away without looking back, or lead them to the door, without making excuses for ending the conversation.

GENERAL ASSERTIVENESS SKILLS FOR CONFLICT MANAGEMENT

- Think about what to say, and what not to say.
- Take responsibility for your anger.
- State your complaint as objectively as possible.
- Be open to criticism.
- Talk about one issue at a time.
- Talk about your anger in private, not in the public domain.
- Don't accuse others of making you angry – use the 'I' word, not the 'you' word:
  'I get angry when …', not 'You make me angry when … '
- Don't be negative. Start with something positive, for example: 'I value our relationship, so want to clear the air.'
- Don't overgeneralise: 'You're always doing …' Be specific.
- Don't shirk your responsibility; acknowledge it.
- Don't put yourself down, or invite retaliatory anger by saying something like, 'I know that I nag …' or 'You'll shout at me when I tell you …'
- Don't bring up past grievances.
- Don't label, mind-read, preach or moralise.
- Don't criticise the person, but their behaviour.
- Don't make idle threats.
- Don't see the resolution as win or lose. Everybody should be a winner.

ACTIVITY

Using any of the skills discussed, write out how to say no with a specific event in mind, *or* choose a situation where you might offer a compromise. In the second scenario, write or make up an entire script stating your compromise, with two alternative endings – firstly, with your compromise accepted and, secondly, where your compromise is not accepted and you have to revert to a no response.

REFLECTION

Consider which model of conflict management you habitually use. If it's the 'destructive' model, reflect on why this might be, and how you could change to the more constructive model. If it seems a very daunting task, ask a trusted Christian friend to pray/think these things through with you.

PRAYER

Loving heavenly Father, I am learning so much; I want to change but some things seem hard and daunting. I ask You to help me overcome my fear, and move on to become the person You created me to be, as I begin to change my 'destructive' pattern to the more 'constructive' model. Thank You that You equip, encourage, and always love me. Amen.

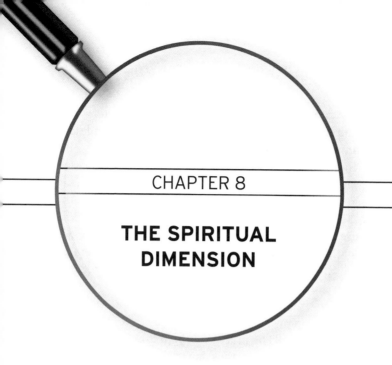

CHAPTER 8

THE SPIRITUAL DIMENSION

May God himself, the God of peace, sanctify you through and through. May your whole spirit, soul and body be kept blameless at the coming of our Lord Jesus Christ. The one who calls you is faithful and he will do it.

(1 Thessalonians 5:23–24)

If you have read this far, it's likely that you have identified yourself, to a greater or lesser extent, as a non-assertive person. Many of us can be assertive at home, where we feel loved, accepted unconditionally and therefore secure. We may even feel in control! Yet outside the home, in any situation where we have to relate to other people, we may find ourselves completely unable to be assertive, fearing rejection or disapproval; we may be totally unable to stand our ground at work, or dislike returning faulty goods to a shop or sending back an unsatisfactory meal in a restaurant, simply because we feel self-conscious and don't want to draw attention to ourselves.

The apostle Paul, struggling with the question of sin in the seventh chapter of his letter to the Christians in Rome, says this: 'I do not understand what I do. For what I want to do I do not do, but what I hate I do' (Rom. 7:15) and goes on, 'For I have the desire to do what is good, but I cannot carry it out. For what I do is not the good I want to do; no, the evil I do not want to do – this I keep on doing' (vv.18b–19). Many of us who are struggling to be assertive can identify with those sentiments.

However, as we have seen, *assertiveness is a skill that can be learnt* – and many who wouldn't call themselves Christians learn assertiveness skills by practising the techniques we've outlined. (It may help that perhaps they don't feel they're letting God or the church down, or being a 'bad witness' by stating what they want or saying no.) So learned techniques and strategies can undoubtedly help. Nevertheless, for a Christian there are solutions that go far deeper than just learning the right skills for otherwise difficult situations. We have alluded to these in earlier chapters, but here we bring them together with the prayer that God will speak to you personally and enable you to make them part of yourself, and so become the whole person that God intends and longs for you to be.

LET GOD FILL YOUR EMOTIONAL TANK

Our Father God, unconditional in His love and acceptance, wants us to know deep down in our innermost beings that each of us is of immense value and worth to Him as an individual. He loved us so much that He sent His Son, Jesus, to live and die for us – and that love, the love that knew us before we were born, that saw us in the womb (Psa. 139:13–16a) still reaches out to us. His Father heart longs for us to run to Him, to pour out our troubles and our sense of inadequacy, and to allow Him to fill us with His love and forgiveness. If we can start here, allowing our innate and God-given need for love and approval to be met by God Himself, then our strategies for dealing with people-pleasing situations will be much more effective.

LEARN TO FEAR GOD MORE THAN PEOPLE

As Christians, it is absolutely vital that we value the person whose acceptance is the most important – our heavenly Father. When we take on board the fact that our value as a person is not dependent upon how we look or what we do, the wound in our self-esteem will begin to heal, and God's unconditional love will help us change our people-pleasing thoughts and behaviour. So many of us are still trying to please our parents, even though we may already be grandparents ourselves! In his book *The Inner Voice of Love*,[1] Henri Nouwen says this:

> Let your father and father figures go … stop seeing yourself through their eyes … you have been a pleaser, depending on others to give you an identity. You need not look at that only in a negative way … [but] let go of all these props and trust that God is enough for you. Stop being a pleaser and reclaim your identity.

It's very easy for Christian people-pleasers to get to a point where they are so bound up with what other people want them to do that God is pushed out. They long for the love and approval of other people more than the love and approval of God. They fear the disapproval of others more than they fear disobeying God. This is a very sad – and a very dangerous – place for a Christian to be in. As we look at the Bible, we can see that from beginning to end runs the message that God asks for first place in our lives, our loves and our allegiances. There are numerous references to loving God more than anyone or anything – Jesus said that no commandment was greater than to 'Love the Lord your God with all your heart and with all your soul and with all your mind and with all your strength' and to 'Love your neighbour as yourself' (Mark 12:30–31).

Sometimes, especially in the Old Testament, the word 'love' is replaced by the word 'fear': we are to fear God. Now, this may seem a little strange in the light of what has been written earlier about unhealthy fears – fear of conflict, fear of rejection, fear of confrontation and so on – but the fear of God that the Bible speaks of is a healthy fear: a sense of awe when we contemplate God's greatness and power … and love. It's awe-inspiring and we don't want to sadden the Father heart of God by not giving Him first place in our lives. So Moses asks the Israelites in Deuteronomy 10:12: '… what does the LORD your God ask of you but to fear the LORD your God …' (see also vv.13–22).

Moses twice exhorted the Israelites as they were crossing the desert, 'learn to fear the LORD' (see Deut. 31:12–13). It's something we have to learn, to pay attention to. Other verses tell us more about this 'fear' of God (with our italics):

- 'The *fear* of the LORD is pure …' (Psa. 19:9)
- 'The *fear* of the LORD is the beginning of wisdom …' (Psa. 111:10)
- 'The *fear* of the LORD teaches a man …' (Prov. 15:33)

- '... delight in the *fear* of the Lord.' (Isa. 11:3)

When we don't fear God (in the biblical sense) more than anyone else, when we don't look to *Him* for our self-worth, we end up trying to seek it from other people; we do this by pleasing them. Then we find ourselves manipulating others, or withdrawing from them altogether. If we love and fear God more than anyone or anything, then we are building on a firm foundation – and, of course, 'fearing' God drives out other fears. Reflect on these wonderfully encouraging verses, and ask God to help you make them part of your 'assertiveness strategy':

Psalm 27:1: 'The Lord is my light and my salvation – whom shall I fear? The Lord is the stronghold of my life – of whom shall I be afraid?'
Psalm 46:1–2: 'God is our refuge and strength, an ever-present help in trouble. Therefore we will not fear, though the earth give way and the mountains fall into the heart of the sea ...'
Romans 8:15: 'For you did not receive a spirit that makes you a slave again to fear, but you received the Spirit of sonship. And by him we cry, "*Abba*, Father."'
Joshua 1:9: 'Have I not commanded you? Be strong and courageous. Do not be terrified; do not be discouraged, for the Lord your God will be with you wherever you go.'
Isaiah 41:13: 'For I am the Lord, your God, who takes hold of your right hand and says to you, Do not fear; I will help you.'

REPENTANCE
Perhaps you recognise yourself somewhere in the preceding paragraphs. What can you do? Repent – which literally means

do an about-turn! Acknowledge with humility that you haven't put God first, that you have been looking in the wrong places for approval and acceptance, or that you have never turned to Him for love and a sense of self-worth. Acknowledge the areas where you fear other people more than you fear God. Admit that your people-pleasing habits have imprisoned you and ask for God's freedom. Ask for His forgiveness and know that He gives it freely. Ask for grace to accept His unconditional love for you, and to live out in your daily life the freedom which that brings. Repentance is making a 180 degree turn, then not just facing in a new direction, but walking along a new path. Repentance needs to be accompanied by action, so it's important to start stepping out using some assertiveness skills.

CONFESSION AND REPENTANCE – STEP BY STEP
There are some simple steps we can take that will help us to become graciously assertive like Jesus.

1. Acknowledge and confess people-pleasing habits
One of Satan's key tactics is to deceive us about the reality of sin. Perhaps you are like the two of us (Chris O and Chris L), and have allowed people-pleasing to develop in your life because you thought people-pleasing was what God wanted? We need to recognise this destructive behaviour for what it is – a despicable thing in God's sight – and then openly and honestly confess this sin to God.

I confess that I have allowed my people-pleasing habits to affect my life and the lives of others. I confess that I have believed my parents'/my pastor's/ others' words that I have to be totally unselfish to be a good Christian.

2. Repent

This involves taking responsibility and saying sorry to God from our hearts and choosing to walk in His ways by becoming assertive. This is about rejecting and renouncing the enemy's lies ('You ought to please everyone!') and choosing to turn back to God.

I am sorry and repent of my ungodly actions and thoughts. I choose to leave my people-pleasing thoughts and habits behind and turn back to You, O God, humbly submitting myself to Your truth.

Then receive God's forgiveness (1 John 1:8–9).

3. Find new freedom by replacing the lies and faulty thinking with God's truth

Choose to align your mind and will with God's truth, and ask Him to continually fill you with the power of His Spirit.

Thank You, Lord, for the grace and favour You pour into my life. I desire to become more assertive but I feel helpless and weak. Therefore I look to You. Please fill me with the power of the Holy Spirit to believe Your truth about me, and help me to learn how to walk in this new way of assertiveness.

Choose to continue living in a new way
Learn:
- To draw on God's love for you.
- To love yourself – 'Love your neighbour *as you love yourself*' (Mark 12:31, NCV, our emphasis).
- To accept that your value doesn't depend upon the things you do.
- To take your 'over-guilty' conscience to God.
- To recognise the inner voice of your own needs.

- To look after your own needs.
- To treat yourself as well as you treat others.
- To acknowledge that you will make mistakes, and accept yourself for making them.
- To give yourself time for 'fun' – for the things you enjoy doing.
- *Not* to pretend that it's OK when people take advantage of you.
- *Not* to compromise godly values, or your own needs or identity as a unique child of God, simply to please other people.

Give yourself permission:
- To say no when appropriate – when it's more important to care for your own needs than for other people's.
- To be honest and real in communicating your opinions, beliefs and feelings – being assertive but not aggressive.
- To change your mind even when this is inconvenient.
- To make decisions that others may find illogical without feeling you have to justify them.
- To state your lack of understanding about a matter without feeling embarrassed.
- *Not* to be 'nice' and a people-pleaser.
- *Not* to feel responsible for finding solutions to others' problems.

Whatever permissions you give yourself, remember to give the same permission to others – so, in allowing yourself to say no to a request, you are giving others permission to say no to your requests.

Remember, too, that turning from being a people-pleaser to being assertive is unlikely to happen overnight; it will take time and there will be setbacks. Forgive yourself and keep at it. Draw on God's love and keep practising the skills and techniques we've outlined in the book.

ACTIVITY

Find a place where you can be comfortable, uninterrupted and still for half an hour. If you find that listening to music helps you relax, play it softly. Ask God to open your spiritual eyes and to speak to you as you read His Word. Then read slowly through Psalm 139 – Chris O finds it helpful to read aloud in this situation. Then read the psalm a second time, putting in your own name where appropriate. Find a particular verse or phrase that you can carry with you as a reminder of what God is saying to you at this important point of your life, where you choose, before God, not to be a people-pleaser any longer. You might find it helpful to write down anything that occurs to you as you read, or to paint or sketch, or to turn your thoughts into prayers. Maybe you would like to write the verse or phrase out and put it on the fridge or on a mirror or in your diary – somewhere where it will remind you of the transaction between you and your heavenly Father.

REFLECTION

Reflect on the fact that God knows you intimately and loves you unboundedly and unconditionally … just as you are. Spend some time basking in the thought that you are so loved. Look at your 'special' verse or phrase and let the words sink deep into your spirit.

PRAYER

Father, thank You that I am so precious, so honoured in Your sight, so loved, so cared for, so esteemed. I am of such great worth and value that You sent Your only Son to die for me so that I can be Your child, Your friend, Your beloved. Praise Your name, Lord. Amen.

NOTES

CHAPTER 1
1. Henry Cloud and John Townsend, *Boundaries: When to Say Yes, How to Say No to Take Control of Your Life* (Grand Rapids, Michigan: Zondervan, 2002).

CHAPTER 2
1. Philip Yancey, *What's So Amazing About Grace?* (Grand Rapids, Michigan: Zondervan, 1997).

CHAPTER 3
1. Philip Yancey, *What's So Amazing About Grace?* (Grand Rapids, Michigan: Zondervan, 1997).
2. Ibid.

CHAPTER 4
1. Windy Dryden and Daniel Constantinou, *Assertiveness Step by Step* (London: Sheldon Press, 2004).
2. Karen Horney, *The Neurotic Personality of our Time* (New York: Norton, 1993).

CHAPTER 5
1. Dennis Wholey, quoted in Harriet B. Braiker, *The Disease to Please* (New York: McGraw-Hill, 2000), p.115.
2. Google 'domestic violence' or look at the following organisations' websites: the National Centre for Domestic Violence: www.ncdv.org.uk or Women's Aid: www.womensaid.org.uk.

CHAPTER 6
1. Harriet B. Braiker, *The Disease to Please* (New York: McGraw-Hill, 2000).
2. Ibid.
3. Wendy Bray and Chris Ledger, *Insight into Anger* (Farnham: CWR, 2007), pp.87–89.

CHAPTER 8
1. Henri J.M. Nouwen, *The Inner Voice of Love: A Journey through anguish to freedom* (London: Darton, Longman and Todd, 1997).

Day and Residential Courses
Counselling Training
Leadership Development
Biblical Study Courses
Regional Seminars
Ministry to Women
Daily Devotionals
Books and Videos
Conference Centre

Trusted all Over the World

CWR HAS GAINED A WORLDWIDE reputation as a centre of excellence for Bible-based training and resources. From our headquarters at Waverley Abbey House, Farnham, England, we have been serving God's people for over 40 years with a vision to help apply God's Word to everyday life and relationships. The daily devotional *Every Day with Jesus* is read by nearly a million readers an issue in more than 150 countries, and our unique courses in biblical studies and pastoral care are respected all over the world. Waverley Abbey House provides a conference centre in a tranquil setting.

For free brochures on our seminars and courses, conference facilities, or a catalogue of CWR resources, please contact us at the following address:
CWR, Waverley Abbey House, Waverley Lane, Farnham, Surrey GU9 8EP, UK

Telephone: **+44 (0)1252 784700**
Email: **mail@cwr.org.uk**
Website: **www.cwr.org.uk**

CWR Applying God's Word
to everyday life and relationships

More insights from our wealth of experience

The *Waverley Abbey Insight Series* brings together biblical understanding and practical advice to offer clear insight, teaching and help on a range of issues.

Insight into Addiction – Find out how addictions take hold and how their power can be destroyed at the roots, never to rise again.
ISBN: 978-1-85345-505-6 **£7.99**

Insight into Anger – Learn how to diagnose the deep roots of inappropriate anger and discover how to overcome resentment, rage and bitterness.
ISBN: 978-1-85345-437-0 **£7.99**

Insight into Anxiety – Discover just what anxiety is, who is at risk of it and how to help those who suffer from it.
ISBN: 978-1-85345-436-3 **£7.99**

Insight into Depression – Discover a holistic and God-centred approach to moving through and beyond depression.
ISBN: 978-1-85345-538-4 **£7.99**

Insight into Forgiveness – Find freedom from the past through the power to forgive, and see how living a life of forgiveness brings release and freedom.
ISBN: 978-1-85345-491-2 **£7.99**

Insight into Perfectionism – Find a balance and enjoy inner rest and peace.
ISBN: 978-1-85345-506-3 **£7.99**

Insight into Bereavement – Find out what emotions arise when a loved one dies, we experience divorce or the loss of a job etc, and learn how to work through the grieving process.
ISBN: 978-1-85345-385-4 **£7.50**

Insight into Eating Disorders – Discover the root causes of eating disorders and deal effectively with the denial and self-destruction that trap most sufferers. Written by a former anorexic and the founder of an eating disorders charity.
ISBN: 978-1-85345-410-3 **£7.50**

Insight into Self-esteem – Cultivate healthy self-esteem by deepening your relationship with God.
ISBN: 978-1-85345-409-7 **£7.50**

Insight into Stress – Recognise stress and its causes, and learn what you can do about it.
ISBN: 978-1-85345-384-7 **£7.50**

Prices correct at time of printing and exclude p&p

Available from CWR by calling **+44 (0)1252 784710**, online at **www.cwrstore.org.uk** – or from your local Christian bookshop.